HEARING CONFESSIONS

HEARING CONFESSIONS

Kenneth Ross

WIPF & STOCK · Eugene, Oregon

Wipf and Stock Publishers
199 W 8th Ave, Suite 3
Eugene, OR 97401

Hearing Confessions
By Ross, Kenneth N.
Copyright©1974 SPCK
ISBN 13: 978-1-62564-925-6
Publication date 5/31/2014
Previously published by SPCK, 1974

Contents

PUBLISHER'S NOTE

The text of this book is, in the main, as Kenneth Ross left it. He died, however, before he had time to revise his script, and it needed some editorial preparation before it could be published. There have been a few omissions, a few additional references have been added, and a very few modifications have been made. This work was done, at the publisher's invitation, by Canon Reginald Cant, Chancellor of York Minster.

ACKNOWLEDGEMENTS

Thanks are due to the following for permission to quote from copyright sources:

Faber and Faber Ltd: *The Descent of the Dove*, by Charles Williams

William Collins, Sons and Co. Ltd and Harper and Row Publishers, Inc.: *I Knew Dietrich Bonhoeffer*, edited by W. D. Zimmerman and R. G. Smith

Cambridge University Press: Essay by Harry Williams in *Soundings*, edited by A. R. Vidler

Hodder and Stoughton Ltd and Word Inc.: *Confess Your Sins*, by J. R. Stott

SCM Press Ltd: *Spirit of Flame: St John of the Cross*, by E. Allison Peers

Darton, Longman and Todd Ltd and Doubleday and Co. Inc.: *Jerusalem Bible*

A memoir of the author

BY GORDON HOPKINS

Canon Residentiary of Durham

Kenneth Needham Ross was born and brought up in Worcester. He was devoted to his parents, who were people of great charm and old-fashioned goodness. Equally, to the end of his life, he was closely attached to his two sisters. The family were very happy and united. Kenneth Ross was an outstandingly able scholar at King's School, Worcester, where there was a good classical tradition. He was head of the school. During these years, T. A. Lacey was a Canon of Worcester. He was a man of deep erudition, and a spiritual director of rare genius and discernment, and a considerable factor in the formation of Kenneth's vocation. As a scholar of the college, this somewhat shy but very able and determined young man quickly made his mark when he came up to Merton College, Oxford. He was the force behind the revival of the Merton Church Society, and I well remember his bringing T. A. Lacey to the college to read a paper on Prayer. After his first in Classical Mods and a second in Greats, Kenneth read the honours school of Theology, and gained a first class honours degree in one year. This was a great achievement even though it involved some measure of strain. During the whole of his time at Merton, K. N. Ross enjoyed the friendship of F. W. Green, who was a fellow, chaplain, and tutor in Theology. He was a vintage Oxford 'character' about whom there are endless stories. He had the gift, there in Oxford, at the same period as Hoskyns in Cambridge, of making Theology an exciting and stimulating academic discipline; and Kenneth Ross never ceased to be grateful for all that 'the Greener' had meant to him.

After a year at Cuddesdon under Eric Graham, Ross was made deacon at Michaelmas 1932, to serve at St Michael's, Radford, Nottingham; he was ordained by the Bishop of Southwell, Bishop Henry Mozley, a friend of F. W. Green. Almost as soon as he was ordained priest, pressure was brought upon the diocese to release him for work as chaplain and tutor at Salisbury theological college. He played a very full part in the life of the college and helped in the parish of St Martin's, Salisbury. At St Martin's he would sometimes preach to the girls of the Godolphin School. At the beginning of the war, Salisbury theological college joined up with Wells, and Kenneth served on the staff of the joint college. The supply of ordination candidates dried up as the war went on, so that Ross readily accepted the offer of a Merton living. This was St John the Baptist, Old Malden. People had thought of him hitherto as being essentially an academic person, learned but somewhat reserved. At Old Malden, it was quickly apparent that he was an immense success as a parish priest. He had always been an able preacher—a consistently good preacher. I can still remember in detail the sermon he preached on the woman of Samaria, from John 4. Liturgically, he was knowledgeable and ordered things very well; pastorally, he was first rate; and here he began his notable work in the confessional. Kenneth never wore his heart on his sleeve : he was the very soul of discretion, and people knew this and they came to him. These three qualities made him the ideal choice as vicar of All Saints', Margaret Street. He was inducted during the Festival of Britain, when London was seething with crowds, and he quickly established his ministry at All Saints'. He had his work cut out. His predecessor, Fr Cyril Tomkinson, was a great 'character'—but the war had told on him, and so had increasing years, and All Saints' needed new life.

Few people are aware of the permanent stress and effort involved in maintaining a great institution at a high pitch of intensity. Everything seemed to go smoothly—yet Kenneth Ross's ministry was costly and sacrificial to a high degree. His confessional in London may be compared with that of Huvelin in Paris. He was never free from financial worries at All Saints', and everything had to be kept going in a rapidly changing post-war world. Kenneth remained impenetrable, but he gained the respect and affection of countless people who owed their very selves to his ministry. The first ten or twelve years of his ministry were very happy and successful; then there came a time of great strain over the inevitable closure of the school. Perhaps another man would have shared the burden, but Fr Ross took and shouldered the whole weight of it, and no one will ever know the extent of the strain which told upon him.

His work at All Saints' was notable, but he was never honoured

by the London diocese, nor was a move forthcoming at a time when
he needed a respite from the weight of his labours until he was
offered a canonry at Wells, where he spent less than a year of utter
happiness. He died in June 1970, after a few days of acute heart
trouble. People in Wells mourned the loss of a great priest, who, in a
short time, was greatly valued.

Kenneth Ross's literary work added up to a considerable total.
Some of his friends would reproach him for never producing a
magnum opus. He would reply that he knew he could write pamph-
lets and books of a popular sort, and was no longer an academic
person.

Although he was somewhat reserved, Kenneth was extremely
good company; he enjoyed a good meal and a convivial evening, and
was a superb *raconteur*. He was a wonderful holiday companion—
a very thorough sightseer. With the help of a *Guide Bleu*, Florence
or Lucca, Brittany or Burgundy, would be seen to the very last
picture or fresco. Latterly, he and his sisters had enjoyed Hellenic
travelling.

His comparatively early death was a great shock to all who knew
and loved him.

1
What this book is about

The scene is St Mary's Church, Barset; the action takes place in a side chapel at 6.30 p.m. on a Saturday evening. A man is kneeling at his devotions; the vestry door opens, and a priest emerges, wearing surplice and purple stole. The priest kneels for a few moments at the altar rails, and then goes to a seat against the wall, beside which there is a kneeling-desk. The man rises to his feet, comes to the kneeling-desk, and kneels. The following dialogue ensues.

PENITENT
Father, give me your blessing, for I have sinned.

PRIEST
The Lord be in your heart and on your lips, that you may truly and humbly confess your sins, in the Name of the Father, and of the Son, and the Holy Spirit. Amen.

PENITENT
I confess to God Almighty, the Father, the Son, and the Holy Spirit, and before the whole company of heaven, that I have sinned exceedingly in thought, word, and deed, by my own grievous fault. My last confession was three months ago.

I have often got up late and consequently rushed or forgotten my morning prayers. Once I failed to say my evening prayers—I was a bit drunk, and it was rather late. Twice I've failed to get to the Parish Communion; once was unavoidable, but the other time I was just being selfish and wanted to get on with something in the garden. Often I've failed to remember God at all in the course of the day. Several times I haven't done my bible reading. I've sometimes been a bit short-tempered with my children, especially my eldest son, and I have been too concerned to criticize rather than to praise. Once I struck my youngest son rather hard. I've been moody with my wife and sometimes enjoyed making her miserable. Once or twice I have expressed my annoyance at being kept waiting before going out. At the office I have sometimes been jealous of one person, and have lost no opportunity of drawing attention to his faults. I have looked at girls with lust in my heart, on one occasion for rather a long time. Twice I have masturbated. I have talked a lot about my successes on the golf course and despised some of my neighbours. I deliberately cut a Fête Committee meeting. I've been a bit unkind when I've talked about my daughter's current boy-friend. I think I've neglected my wife a bit, going out to do things for other people.

For these and all my other sins which I cannot now remember I am heartily sorry, firmly mean to do better, and humbly ask pardon of God, and of you, father, penance, counsel and absolution.

PRIEST

When we find ourselves getting slack, it isn't always enough just to say 'I must turn over a new leaf'. We know we ought to, but so often we don't really want to. So think a bit more of God's love for you, really listen to scripture, really attend to your reading of it in this connection and think of the way in which you are indebted to your wife and family for so many blessings. Don't take them for granted, but express your appreciation to them from time to time. Remember in connection with your daughter that you are probably a bit jealous of her boyfriend; most fathers resent being cut out in their daughters' affections, and it shows itself in odd ways. As your penance, will you say the General Thanksgiving?—Oh, and don't necessarily feel badly about cutting the occasional meeting. It's different if your presence is vital. You have to use your discretion in these matters.

Almighty God have mercy upon you, forgive you your sins, and bring you to everlasting life.

The almighty and merciful God grant you pardon and remission of all your sins.

Our Lord Jesus Christ, who has left power to his Church to absolve all sinners who truly repent and believe in him, of his great mercy forgive you your offences; and by his authority committed to me, I absolve you from all your sins ✠ in the Name of the Father and of the Son and of the Holy Spirit. Amen.

The Passion of our Lord Jesus Christ and his infinite merits be to you for the remission of sins, the increase of grace, and the reward of everlasting life.

And the blessing of God Almighty, the Father, the Son, and the Holy Spirit, be upon you, and remain with you always.

Go in peace. The Lord has put away your sins. And pray for me, a sinner.

The man rises and goes back to his place. He takes up a Prayer Book, reads the General Thanksgiving silently, and also Psalm 103. Then he kneels thoughtfully for a while. Before leaving the church he puts a couple of coins in the alms box. Meanwhile the priest has risen and knelt at the altar rail, before returning to the vestry.

2

A brief historical and theological sketch

One of the things which differentiate Christians today from those who lived in the first generation of Christianity is that they were vividly aware of living in the last times. The axe was laid to the root of the trees; God's kingly rule was in their midst in the person of Jesus Christ; and if he was withdrawn from their sight, it was only for a little while—he would return in the same manner as he had left the earth. Much of his teaching had a 'now or never' tone to it, and he taught his followers to pray a prayer which was full'of urgency. It was that the heavenly Father would make his decisive intervention in human history, that he would sanctify his name, establish his kingdom, and effect his purpose. Poised on the edge of this great event, his followers were to pray to be fed even today with the bread of the great tomorrow, to ask for acquittal from him who was appointed judge on the last day, and to pray that in the great testing-time which would usher in the last day they might be spared, and not fall into the hands of the evil one.[1]

The Church was a group with a limited period in which to do its work. Paul was inclined to advise his unmarried converts at Corinth not to marry in view of the shortness of the time, unless the urge to do so was very strong. There seems to have been little or no idea of the Church as an institution continuing down the centuries; rather, the time was short, and 'I come quickly' seemed to be the promise and the warning of the risen Lord. Baptism united the believer to the dying and rising again of Jesus, and was a symbolic enactment of death and resurrection; the Eucharist was the interim meal of believers 'till he come'; and 'Maranatha' or 'Come, Lord' was the constantly repeated prayer.

As time went on, different insights emerged. St John's Gospel, while still looking forward to the future consummation, places the

[1] See Ernst Lohmeyer, *The Lord's Prayer* (Collins 1965).

emphasis on the present reality of what is still future. 2 Peter, generally dated now in the first half of the second century, admits that some people are disillusioned and cynical as a result of the delayed appearance of the Lord; his answer is to say that what is 'soon' for God may be a very long time for man, and that the delay in any case is to ensure that as many people as possible are saved first.

It is necessary to weigh all this if one is to grasp what is involved in the forgiveness of sins. Just as the eye of faith saw the final resurrection present when Jesus raised a dead man to life, so the eye of faith saw the last judgement in operation when he forgave a sinner his sins; here already was the judge of living and dead. Baptism was a sacrament of the last times; for the reconciled sinner judgement was past and over, he was reborn for the resurrection. In a time of crisis there is no leisure for making fine distinctions: a man is either for the truth or against it, he is either loyal or a traitor. So to turn one's back on the truth after accepting it was to be guilty of the gravest possible sin. The writer of Hebrews says roundly, 'It is impossible for them to be renewed a second time' (6.6); like Esau they have made their choice, and they must suffer for it (12.17). The writer may well not have faced the question which interests the modern reader—was the 'impossibility' of renewal subjective or objective? Was it due to the fact that they had finally rejected Christ, or to the fact that the Church had no remedy to cure such sinners, even if they did repent?

Wherever Jesus was, there were the last times, and by delegation this was to be true of his followers also. 'As the Father sent me, so am I sending you' (John 20.21). 'Receive the Holy Spirit. For those whose sins you retain, they are retained' (20.22-3). Christ addressed these words to 'the disciples', which may or may not denote the apostles. But the solemn 'sending' of v. 21 strongly suggests that it denotes only the apostles (whether these are a larger body than the Twelve or not). Whatever it may mean, it is not just a command to preach forgiveness in general terms: there is to be some sort of careful discrimination. Jesus himself forgave particular individuals in virtue of the authority which he possessed as Son of man (Mark 2.10), but this was not an authority which he exercised autocratically: 'the Son can do nothing by himself; he can only do what he sees the Father doing' (John 5.19). Similarly the authority handed on to the apostles by the risen Lord is subject to a similar limitation;

all must be in his name and in accordance with his will.

It is in this way that the Church understands the commission to Peter to bind and loose (Matt. 16.19) and the similar commission to the apostles corporately (Matt. 18.18): they are to apply the Lord's principles with the aid of the Lord's discretion—the Holy Spirit. The baptism of the Gentile Cornelius is a notable example (Acts 10.44-8); the apostolic decree is another (Acts 15.28-9). More immediately relevant is the case of the incestuous man at Corinth, and how Paul—and the Church—dealt with it (1 Cor. 5.1-5). It is all part of 'Anyone who listens to you, listens to me' (Luke 10.16), and 'Teach them to observe all the commands I gave you. And know that I am with you always; yes, to the end of time' (Matt. 28.20).

There have been different opinions about the pattern to be found in the New Testament. One extreme can be found in the treatment of penance by Thomas Aquinas. Starting with its existence as an acknowledged sacrament, he found its origin in the Gospels: the Lord had said, 'Do penance', according to Jerome's translation (it is more accurately translated, 'Repent' (Matt. 4.17)); and he had instituted the sacrament formally when after the resurrection he pointed the disciples to the fact that the Old Testament showed 'that in his name repentance for the forgiveness of sins would be preached to all the nations' (Luke 24.47). Even combined with the charge, 'Those whose sins you forgive, they are forgiven' (John 20.22) this seems an inadequate basis for the explicit institution of a sacrament.

On the other hand, it is equally lacking in plausibility to maintain that the charge to forgive sins was only 'a dramatic figure of speech', that the apostles received 'not an authority to forgive, but to preach forgiveness'.[2] It is hard to read Paul's letters to the Corinthians without finding examples of the retaining and forgiving of sin. The truth is that the one extreme provokes the other. It is better to abandon the attempt to justify modern practice by reading what one wishes into the New Testament, and instead to read what the New Testament actually says, admitting that it does not say as much as one might wish, and that what it does say is not as clear as one might wish.

If the Epistle to the Hebrews does imply a rigorist attitude to the apostate, this may well have been typical of the general position of

[2] J. R. W. Stott, *Confess your Sins*, pp. 61-2.

Jewish Christianity; they may have been driven to it in order to counteract the dangers of the Gentile penetration of the Church. Others were less intransigent. Even the author of 1 John, who speaks of a 'deadly sin' (5.16) about which he does not counsel prayer, and who says categorically, 'Anyone who has been begotten by God does not sin' (5.18), in fact takes a milder position than these words might suggest, torn from their context. For he also says, 'If we say we have no sin in us, we are deceiving ourselves and refusing to admit the truth' (1.8), and he specially mentions 'deadly sin' in order to point out that 'not all sin is deadly' (5.17) and that prayer can restore such a sinner.

Serious lapses must have been more common among Gentile Christians, who were subjected to severer pressures from paganism in daily life. Paul had a high doctrine of baptism and expressed horror at the idea of a Christian living a life of sin. But he is pastorally concerned for the sinner, whose predicament he can understand, and if he is cruel it is in order to be kind. The offender should be sent to Coventry, to bring him to his senses (2 Thess. 3.14), but there should be no self-righteousness about it (Gal. 6.1).

Like any other founder of a church, Paul had to wrestle with problems of discipline. 2 Cor. 2.1-11 refers to one such. 'Someone has been the cause of pain' (5), and Paul felt obliged to demand stern action (3.10). This, despite a minority which felt otherwise, was forthcoming (6). Consequently Paul now wishes justice to give place to mercy (7). The Corinthian church must forgive the person in question (7); Paul endorses their forgiveness and the form which it takes, not merely personally but officially (10). The case is of special interest, since Paul is obviously anxious that his forgiveness should be known to be Christ's and to be expressed by the family of Christ at Corinth. The apostle's absolution is official rather than merely personal; he acts in the name of Christ and in the name of his Church.

Some have guessed that the offender in question is the man referred to in 1 Cor. 5.1-8. Here is a man who has committed incest. Paul directs that he is to be solemnly excommunicated : this sentence has his authorization and is in the name of Christ. The offender is 'to be handed over to Satan' (4) in the expectation that this will result in his sickness and death—and, as a result, his ultimate salvation. If the two passages refer to the same person, it is clear that the sharp sentence had a salutary effect. Paul feels able now to lift the curse and to restore the now penitent sinner to fellowship.

The Pastoral Epistles give the same picture: sometimes excommunication is necessary (1 Tim. 1.20), or public rebuke, even of a presbyter (1 Tim. 5.20). It is possible that the laying on of hands as a sign of restoration to fellowship is referred to in 1 Tim. 5.22, though others interpret this as referring to ordination.

The Epistle of James has special interest, since it associates the confession of sins with anointing with oil in sickness (5.14-16). The purpose of these exercises here mentioned is bodily healing. The passage reads as though it is the presbyters who will be concerned not only in the anointing but in the receiving of the sick man's confession. But 'confess your sins to one another, and pray for one another' (5.16) may have a wider reference.

The letters to the seven churches in Revelation contain many exhortations to repent, with no hint that forgiveness is impossible for any sinner; but clearly it is envisaged that many of those cut off as a punishment from the Christian community will remain outside, since judgement day is so close.

But do not the Gospels show that Jesus taught that there is such a thing as an unforgivable sin? This is so, but the Gospels preserve different traditions about what it is. Mark (3.28-30) tells how Jesus declared all sins, even against God, to be forgivable, with the exception of blasphemy against the Holy Spirit, and he explains why Jesus said this: 'This was because they were saying an unclean spirit is in him.' In other words, since the opponents of Jesus were of deliberate malice attributing the works of God to the Devil, they had irrevocably identified themselves with the powers of darkness: they cannot be forgiven, because they refuse to admit that there is anything to forgive. Matt. (12.31-2) and Luke (12.10) know the saying in a different form: blasphemy against the Son of Man is forgivable, but not blasphemy against the Holy Spirit. Presumably this means that to misunderstand who Jesus is and to reject him is forgivable, but wilfully to take good for evil is not.

The fear of having committed 'the unforgivable sin' has haunted people in the past (a famous example in fiction may be found in George Borrow's Lavengro, together with the wise counsel which dissipated this fear) and still does occasionally today. Anyone who despairs needs to be told that if he is penitent he cannot have committed the unforgivable sin, and that the Lord's promise still holds good, 'Whoever comes to me I shall not turn him away' (John 6.37).

During the last fifty years there has been a notable recovery of the doctrine of the Church as the Body of Christ, and consequently of the sacraments not merely and not primarily as establishing a relationship between the believer and God, but as something corporate and having to do with the life of the whole Christian community. In baptism sins are forgiven so that the individual may find new birth with the life of the new community of the Church, and in the Eucharist the receiving of the sacrament serves to deepen and strengthen the supernatural life of the community. It is important to see the reconciliation of the sinner as primarily the work of the Christian community. A man is cut off from the fellowship of the community, if his sin is a grave one, and is once again restored. Both actions are formal and official, pronounced in the name of the community by its leaders, and both carry with them the divine endorsement. The man who is excommunicated should see in his separation from the community an experience of the outer darkness, and when he is restored he should experience the joy of being restored into the favour of God himself.

There is a great deal to be learned from a study of the various ways in which the Church throughout its history has used this power of reconciliation. One can begin to see future methods by which both the eschatological and the corporate aspects can be given greater prominence than in recent centuries. What is vain is to try to find examples of the modern atomized and individualistic absolution either in the New Testament or in the records of the early Church. The Catholic need not regard the appeal to Scripture as Protestant or the appeal to history as treachery, simply because it is hard to find in Scripture or history the distorted sacramentalism of the nineteenth century; and the Protestant need not feel that he has disposed of sacramental confession when he triumphantly demonstrates the absence of the nineteenth-century form of it from the pages of Scripture. For both Catholic and Protestant can recover the fullness of truth from patient study of Bible and history.

Even in the first century the Church began to adapt itself to new circumstances. Her own existence seemed likely to be much longer than was originally thought. But there was another adaptation which was made, and this has sometimes been criticized as a betrayal of the gospel. To an ever-decreasing extent the Church could assume the existence of Jewish standards of morality and religion and show the way in which its own gospel transcended them—law was not the last word, for grace was supreme. More and more it was the case that there was little acceptance of ordinary moral standards, and in such a situation it was dangerous for Christian preachers to announce the supersession of moral laws by the gospel of Jesus Christ. The Church had simultaneously to teach and enforce ordinary moral standards and to proclaim the fact that they were transcended by the gospel. Something of the same situation confronts the Church today. It is not surprising if a proper balance between these two most necessary tasks is not always preserved. In the second century, most of people's energies went on trying to secure the acceptance of a reasonably high level of ordinary behaviour. It remains to be seen what will be the effect today of devoting the smaller amount of time and consideration to that task.

It is exceptionally difficult to unravel what was taught and what was done in those early centuries, for the evidence is scanty and can be interpreted in different ways. Take for example that important book, the *Shepherd* of Hermas. The usual explanation of it is that in a context in which rigorism had hitherto prevailed, it announced the special concession on one occasion only of a reconciliation with the Church of those who had sinned gravely since their baptism.[3] But others have thought the context to have been more liberal, and believe that Hermas marked a reaction towards rigorism, and that he was limiting reconciliation to one occasion.[4] What is incontrovertible is the wrestling of the Church with the constant tension between rigorism and liberalism, and the first occurrence of the familiar pastoral dilemma, how to give hope to the believer who has sinned, without thereby implicitly offering encouragement to other believers to commit sin.

Even when he was orthodox, Tertullian was rigorist in temperament, and preferred to exclude the penitent rather than give any handle to sin. He almost apologized for post-baptismal reconciliation.

Though the great gate of forgiveness has been barred and bolted at baptism, second penance waits in the vestibule to open a postern door once more to those who knock. But once more only, for it is the second time; never again, if this once fails (*On Repentance*, chap. viii).

[3] K. E. Kirk, *The Vision of God*, pp. 165-73.
[4] B. Poschmann, *Penance and the Anointing of the Sick*, pp. 26-35.

As a Catholic he appears to have regarded murder, adultery, and apostasy as unforgivable (though this is disputed); as a Montanist he certainly denied the possibility of reconciliation for *any* mortal sin.

While logic drove Tertullian one way, it drove the Catholic Church the other. Whether or not there was a universal ban on the reconciliation of murderers, adulterers, and apostates, it certainly operated in some parts of the Church, and at first there was indignation when those who had committed sexual sins were reconciled after penance; but later the same indulgence was shown towards the two other categories.

Modern Christians would regard it as a strange 'indulgence', for severe penitential exercises were required of those who sought reconciliation. Fasting, prayer, abstinence from sexual intercourse and pleasures of every kind, almsgiving—these were only a few of the signs of penitence which were expected. Such penitents formed a well-defined group, for which the prayers of the faithful were implored. This was hard enough, if it was a way of life willingly accepted as a token of sorrow; but before long it changed its character and became rather a penalty for wrongdoing. Worse still, it became possible to view such punishment as making some sort of atonement or satisfaction for one's offences. The severity was such that very few people indeed ever accepted such penance voluntarily; if accepted at all, it would be on a man's deathbed. Linked with this was the prudential deferring of baptism as long as possible; by this means one avoided doing penance for one's grave sins !

Such severity was doomed to failure. Fewer and fewer people submitted themselves to it. It had come to what Bernhard Poschmann calls

> a dead end. The increasing rigidity of its forms had gradually conducted it to the utopian objective of obliging all the faithful sooner or later to a kind of monastic renunciation of the world.... Precisely in the years when sins importuned men most strongly, there was no sacramental remedy at their disposal (*Penance and the Anointing of the Sick*, p. 123).

Slowly changes took place. Augustine had ceased to require the public admission of sin before readmission to communion, since there was a danger of offenders being apprehended by the imperial police and punished. Further, with the weakening of the forces of law and order the bishops became more and more concerned with the ordinary administration of justice, and penances became increasingly penal in character, and assessed to fit the crime rather than the criminal. In the prevailing circumstances this could hardly have been avoided, but it meant that the juridical aspect of the ministry was overemphasized, and this continued, even though various mitigations helped to redress the balance. Severe penalties were reduced in order to be more workable; monetary fines could sometimes be substituted —there was great danger in this; and, scarcely less dangerous, a theoretical basis to justify a more merciful approach was found in the notion of a treasury of merit, on the basis of which the heroic actions of the saints were credited to sinners. The stress is on heavy penalties in this life and in purgatory in the next, and then on the possibility of escaping both by a sufficiently large contribution of money to the Church. It is unnecessary for more to be said here about these lamentable ideas.

There was a marked tendency to make Lent the period of special discipline for the penitents; the fact that a number of people were undergoing penance together must have been a help for the ordinary person. But simultaneously it was a widespread custom for all to accept a voluntary time of penance during Lent. In both cases reconciliation would take place on Maundy Thursday. This markedly penitential character of Lent is the reason for many customs surviving to the present day such as the ashes of Ash Wednesday and the Lenten veiling.

It would take too long to describe the effect of the growth of monasticism on the matter under discussion. It was within monastic communities that the admonition to 'confess your sins to one another' (James 5.16) chiefly bore fruit—the confession itself was the valuable ascetic practice, and often there was no question of absolution. But sometimes, especially in the East, absolution was given after private confession, and by lay monks and deacons as well as by priests. A system like this was well fitted to take the place of one of public penance, which was being less and less used, though it inherited the juridical approach and the tariff method of assigning penances, even though the wiser teachers were insistent that the confessor's task was to deal with people rather than with sins. Normally now the reconciliation took place at once, at the time of the confession, and any penance was performed afterwards rather than beforehand.

With the diminution of the penance and the compounding of it in various ways, there came to be greater stress on the priestly work of absolution. In earlier days the emphasis had rather been laid on the penitent's own contrition and on the raising of the discipline which had been imposed. As the Middle Ages progressed, penance becomes increasingly thought of as a sacrament, and the theologians debated among themselves how to define its matter and form. Was the *matter* the laying on of the priest's hands in absolution? (Alexander of Hales). Were the words of absolution both *form* and *matter*? (Duns Scotus). Are the penitent's contrition, confession, and satis-faction the *quasi-matter*? (Thomas Aquinas). The Council of Trent endorsed the last of these views, but the question is not really settled in the Roman Catholic Church even now.

Thus at the time of the Reformation there was the institution of public penance for grave and public offences; there was the obligation, imposed in 1215, on all to make a yearly confession before receiving the sacrament at Easter; there was freedom to do more than this, to seek absolution at any time for sin whether mortal or venial.[5]

It had always been maintained that the one condition for receiving the divine forgiveness was true contrition. Nothing could substitute for this, and no sacerdotal interposition was needed in order to secure God's pardon. Perhaps for this reason the priest prayed for the penitent's pardon; only in the twelfth century and only in the West did the priest authoritatively declare the penitent forgiven ('I absolve thee'). But the unique need for contrition was obscured by the teaching that for forgiveness a man needed not only contrition but also the intention to use the sacrament of penance. Though the latter was not intrinsically necessary, it had become necessary since the Church had ruled that everyone should use it once a year. There was a marked tendency to suggest that one could not be certain of forgiveness unless one had used the sacrament of penance. For if one is in a state of sin, how can one obtain the grace of contrition, which is the one thing necessary? Thus in practice sacramental absolution becomes necessary in order to ensure contrition; and theologians long disputed whether the imperfect contrition known as *attrition* justified the conferring of absolution.

These technical disputes are of interest to the specialist. What needs to be pointed out is that different writers mean very different things by their terms, *contrition* and *attrition*, with the result that people who seem to be saying the opposite to one another are often

[5] See pp. 37-40 for a discussion of this distinction.

meaning the same thing. For this reason attacks on the doctrine of the adequacy of attrition in the sixteenth and seventeenth centuries need to be read with discrimination. There is plenty of common ground between the two extremes, of believing that making one's confession with some sort of regret for sin eliminated any need for genuine contrition, and of so insisting on the pure love of God as a prerequisite for forgiveness as to put it out of reach for the majority of people. The experience of St Alphonsus quoted on p. 24 explains the pastoral concern of those who would not wish to quench the smoking flax: though inadequately contrite at the start, by the time they are absolved they have become contrite.

What needs to be noted is the long-continued uncertainty within the Church of the rationale of the sacrament of penance. The medi-aeval debates on the subject were long and bitter; and unfortunately the view of Thomas Aquinas which soon became dominant was seriously defective. On the one hand, he believed that contrition won forgiveness from God; on the other hand, he believed that absolution conferred contrition. If then a penitent had perfect contrition before sacramental confession, his forgiveness was due to the sacrament which operated pre-emptively, since such a penitent was necessarily intending in obedience to the Church to seek sacramental absolution. This is artificial. It is connected also with his view that the result of absolution was contrition, rather than reconciliation with the Church. Such reconciliation is itself the sign and pledge of the divine forgiveness.

The practice of the Orthodox Church in relation to sacramental confession is in contrast to what has been characteristic of the Roman Catholic Church (cf. p. 64). It has always emphasized the corporate aspect of the sacrament and the penitent's reconciliation with the community. Commonly before making his confession the penitent would go round the members of his household and family and ask their forgiveness for wrongs done; then he would seek out his priest in church. As regards the administration of the sacrament, both priest and penitent stand, and this emphasizes the fact that the priest is both a fellow sinner and a witness of the confession representing the local church.

Orthodox writers often claim that the priest acts as physician of the soul and not as judge, and it is true that his role is largely that of compassionate and prudent adviser and doctor. There is no stress on the power of the keys, but it is none the less presupposed, and

Orthodox writers say, just as Western writers do, that the priest needs to know what the penitent's sins are before he can exercise the power of binding and loosing. Though penances may be imposed, this is not regarded as necessary and is in practice comparatively rare. Much is left to the initiative and tact of the priest, and there are wide divergences of practice both among priests of the same Church, and between different Orthodox Churches. In the Russian Church, Holy Communion will not be given unless the would-be communicant has first made his confession and been absolved; but in other Churches confession is only required after grave sin. It needs to be remembered that in most parts of the Orthodox Church the reception of Holy Communion is infrequent.

One welcome emphasis is that confession is to the Lord Jesus himself. For too long in the practice of the Roman Catholic Church it has seemed as if the penitent told his sins to the priest and received priestly absolution. True, he has made an act of contrition to God and he has usually had a crucifix before his eyes as he made his confession; but it has often been more of a human judicial transaction than a meeting with the merciful Saviour. The words with which the Orthodox priest addresses the penitent before the confession are worth noting:

Behold, my son, Christ is invisibly present to receive your confession. Therefore do not be ashamed or afraid, and conceal nothing from me, but tell me without equivocation what you have done. So you shall have pardon from our Lord Jesus Christ. See, his image is before us. I am only a witness to bear testimony before him of all you say to me. But if you conceal anything from me, you will have double sin; so take care, since you come for medicine, lest you go away unhealed.

The fullest exposition of the Church of England's teaching on confession and absolution is to be found in the exhortation in the 1549 Prayer Book (which in a changed form became the first of three in the Prayer Book of 1662). Much as in the 1662 form it teaches self-examination and repentance, and then proceeds:

And if there be any of you whose conscience is troubled and grieved in anything, lacking comfort or counsel, let him come to me, or to some other discreet and learned priest, taught in the law of God, and confess and open his sin and grief secretly, that he

may receive such ghostly counsel, advice and comfort, that his
conscience may be relieved, and that of us (as of the ministers of
God and of the Church) he may receive comfort and absolution,
to the satisfying of his mind, and avoiding of all scruple and
doubtfulness; requiring such as shall be satisfied with a general
confession not to be offended with them that do use, to their further
satisfying, the auricular and secret confession to the priest; nor
those also which think needful or convenient, for the quietness of
their own consciences, particularly to open their sins to the priest,
to be offended with them that are satisfied with their humble
confession to God and the general confession to the church. But in
all things to follow and keep the rule of charity, and every man
to be satisfied with his own conscience, not judging other men's
minds or consciences; whereas he hath no warrant of God's Word
to the same.

All may: none must. But also, *some should*; and it was recognized
that a sick person should make his confession if his conscience was
troubled with any weighty matter (*Visitation of the Sick*, 1549 and
1552).

There is abundant evidence that many did avail themselves of
this means of grace. Richard Hooker confessed on his deathbed to
Hadrian à Saravia, and Confessors to the Royal Household fulfilled
the function for which they were appointed throughout the seventeenth century. Archbishops of Canterbury commended the practice,
not only William Laud, regarded by some of his contemporaries as
papistical, but the liberal William Wake; in his *Exposition of the
Doctrine of the Church of England* he wrote:

We exhort men, if they have any the least doubt or scruple, nay
sometimes, though they have not, but especially before they
receive the Holy Sacrament to confess their sins. We propose to
them the benefit not only of ghostly advice how to manage their
repentance, but the great comfort of absolution as soon as they
shall have completed it. When we visit our sick, we never fail
to exhort them to make a special confession of their sins to him
that ministers to them; and when they have done it, the absolution
is so full, that the Church of Rome itself could not desire to add
anything to it.

Canon 19 of the Church of Ireland (1634) required that on the afternoon before the celebration of Holy Communion warning should be given

> by tolling of the bell, or otherwise, to the intent that if any have any scruple or conscience, or desire the special ministry of reconciliation, he may afford it to those that need it. And to this end the people are often to be exhorted to enter into a special examination of the state of their own souls; and that finding themselves either extremely dull or much troubled in mind, they do resort unto God's ministers, to receive from them as well advice and counsel for the quickening of their dead hearts and the subduing of those corruptions whereunto they have been subject, as the benefit of absolution likewise, for the quieting of their consciences, by the power of the keys which Christ hath committed to his ministers for that purpose.

But it was not until the Prayer Book of 1662 that it was explicitly stated that *some should*, as well as the fact that *all may* and *none must*. For the rubric in *The Visitation of the Sick* was changed in order to lay upon the priest the duty of urging a detailed confession of sins on any sick person whose conscience was troubled as a result of grievous sin. 'Here shall the sick person be moved to make a special confession of his sins, if he feel his conscience troubled with any weighty matter. After which confession the priest shall absolve him (if he humbly and heartily desire it) after this sort.' Even in the case of the uneasy conscience, though confession is to be urged, absolution is not to be forced on the sick man; but if it is given, the words are exactly prescribed. John Stott is in error in supposing that 'after this sort' means, 'in some such words as these';[6] it means, 'in this way'. Earlier in the Order provision is made for variety in an unambiguous way: 'Here shall the minister exhort the sick person after this form, or other like'.

Incidental remarks in the novels of Fielding and Smollett make it plain that the teaching of the Prayer Book embedded itself in the popular mind. This is the more noteworthy since Fielding was a Low Churchman and Smollett was a Presbyterian. However, unsupernatural religion was characteristic of the eighteenth century, and an Archbishop of Canterbury, Thomas Secker, remarked in a sermon that sacramental confession and absolution were unusual, but 'when-

[6] Op. cit., p. 66.

ever people think it necessary, we are ready both to hear them with the utmost secrecy, and to assist them with our best care; to direct them how they may be forgiven, if we think they are not; to pronounce them forgiven, if we think they are'.[7]

The Tractarian leaders did their best to revive the practice; it was part of their loyalty to the Prayer Book. When, somewhat provocatively, nearly five hundred priests petitioned the Canterbury Convocation to consider the desirability of training and licensing confessors, the main result was to rally the opposition, and the bishops firmly decided not to do any such thing. A few years later they made no effort to expound the traditional teaching when violent attacks on it were made in the House of Lords. However, the violence miscarried, and an Evangelical, George Howard Wilkinson, felt obliged to deliver and print two sermons on the subject which defended the Anglican position.[8]

The way in which opposition abated can be seen in the life of the second Lord Halifax (1839–1934). When he became a penitent in his twenties, his mother wrote him a letter in which she said, 'What has hurt your father more than anything has been that a son of his should go to confession.' Twenty-one years later she herself made her confession, and continued the practice until her death. Out of regard for the feelings of the first Viscount the subject was always avoided; but some time after his wife's death the old man suddenly said to his friend, W. J. Knox-Little, 'You once told me a story of a man who had sent for you to hear his confession: I want to make mine'.[9]

In fairness, however, to those who opposed (and oppose) the practice, it should be pointed out that zealous Anglo-Catholics not infrequently espoused the extreme Roman Catholic position about the *necessity* of sacramental confession for the forgiveness of mortal sin committed after baptism, as well as the basis in dogma on which that conclusion was based. Richard Hooker was right to deny the antiquity of the private confession which had become normal. So it could only become necessary if the Church declared that it was necessary, and the Church had no right to add to the requirements of the gospel.

[7] *Sermons on several subjects*, 1771, vol. VI, sermon xiv (quoted in J. Wickham Legg, *English Church Life from the Restoration to the Tractarian Movement* (1914), p. 275).

[8] In 1874, cf. A. J. Mason, *Memoir of George Howard Wilkinson.*

[9] J. G. Lockhart, *Charles Lindley, Viscount Halifax*, vol. I, pp. 97, 266-7.

All may: none must: some should. Of his friar Chaucer wrote:

> Full sweetly heard he confession,
> And pleasant was his absolution.[10]

He will have welcomed many penitents, who were glad to come to him. Yet there are also those who are drawn to make their confession because it is so much against the grain—and who will say that they are wrong? It was John Donne, that great Dean of St Paul's Cathedral, who wrote in one of his sermons:

> If any man do think that that which is necessary for him upon his death-bed, is necessary every time he comes to Communion, and so come to such a confession if anything lie upon him, we blame not, we dissuade not, we discounsel not, that tenderness of conscience and that safe proceeding in that good soul.... The more I find confession or any religious practice repugnant to mine own nature, the further will I go in it.[11]

Donne was a man of unique sensibility, but he has a point of substance. It is admitted that sacramental confession is not a necessity, it is not required of the individual. But what is the question which the devout individual should ask himself? Not, Do I want to make my confession?, but rather, Ought I to make my confession? Whether I want to or don't want to is immaterial: the point is, what is it that God wants me to do?

[10] *The Canterbury Tales*, The Prologue, ll. 221-2 (Oxford edn 1920, ed. W. W. Skeat).
[11] A sermon preached to the household at Whitehall, April 30, 1626.

3
The priest's role in confession

The complexity of the priest's task in dealing with the sinner is due to the fact that he has to play several parts simultaneously and has to reconcile what sometimes seem to be conflicting interests.

For example, he does his work as the representative of God; he is also the representative of the Church; and he is also there to serve the interests of the penitent sinner to the utmost of his ability. These different roles are liable to pull him in different directions. If on a particular issue the will of God seems unmistakably clear, if the Scriptures make a particular moral issue clear, then it would seem to be his duty to press this upon the penitent, regardless of uncertainties which may exist in the Church on the subject, and regardless of the different way in which the penitent views the issue. In the early Church it was widely thought that it was impossible for a Christian who fell away and denied the faith to be reconciled: it was 'a sin unto death'. As against that, it came to be seen that in practice the welfare of the Church required that this position should be modified; when Christians were a persecuted minority, it was a pity to make unnecessary enemies, and even a weak and unreliable adherent was some help: why not make a special concession in view of the dangers threatening, and close the ranks—why not readmit those who technically were thought to be disqualified for this indulgence? Further, as the complexities of the human heart and the greater awareness of social and psychological pressures became more evident, it became clear that each individual case needed to be considered separately; what viewed from outside seemed a sin of the utmost gravity might be comparatively small in fact, when the actual circumstances had been taken into consideration. Whatever Scripture might say, and whatever the traditional discipline of the Church might be, it might be clear that the guilt of the individual concerned was very small indeed, and that he was therefore entitled to receive the relief which he so much desired.

In more recent times there has been a welcome change of mind about the treatment of those who attempt to commit suicide. Suicide is still regarded as a sin of the utmost gravity; some think that the reprobation of it by the Church is a valuable piece of testimony to a careless world; but it is now widely recognized that in very many cases it is impossible to adjudge that the person concerned had a high rating of guilt; rather it might be infinitesimal. So the problem is to decide how to balance the objective gravity of a sin against the relatively small gravity of the particular action viewed subjectively from the position of the individual concerned.

The Roman Catholic Church is currently concerned with the same type of problem on the issue of contraception. It might seem as though the right way to proceed was obvious, at least for those who believe that Scripture and/or the natural law unequivocally condemn the practice. It might seem as though a priest's duty was to say, 'Here is the truth; obey it, or get out!', and some indeed have taken just this line. But even if the condemnation of contraception were sound in theory, there is still the question of squaring this with the fact that a respectable and conscientious body of opinion within the Church takes a less negative view—if there is a sizeable minority opinion on a subject, is not the individual entitled to follow it? Further, if an individual, having examined the whole question with the greatest care, is sure that contraception is right, or right for him in his particular circumstances, is it not his moral duty, as a Roman Catholic of integrity, to follow his conscience, and, whether objectively his conscience is right or wrong, is he not guiltless in the sight of God and therefore not to be repelled?

This is not an argument for liberalism. The most tolerant view is not always the right view, and no individual member of a society like the Church can claim to believe and do what he likes, regardless of anyone else. The Church has declined to recognize as her children people who deviated from the faith entrusted to her. She may not always have exercised that discretion wisely, but that she is right to exercise it can hardly be disputed. To believe in God and to believe in the resurrection of Jesus Christ is obviously necessary for membership in the Church; some would think it less necessary to believe in the virginal conception of Jesus; many would think it unnecessary to believe in Mary's corporal assumption. Different Christian bodies assess the situation differently. And in matters of morals there is a similar consensus on certain fundamentals; membership of the Church must be denied to a man who believes in his right to be cruel, dishonest, or sexually promiscuous. Whether a belief in the right to remarriage after a divorce should exclude a man is less clear, and whether the fact of remarriage after a divorce should do so is less clear still. It is no good isolating the case of the individual and seeking the best solution for him as an individual; the interests of the community have also to be considered. For the Church, like a school, is a community. In a school the headmaster may know that so far as a particular boy is concerned, he was likely to fare worse away from the school than within it; yet he may feel that the benefit to the boy of remaining at the school was outweighed by the probable harm done to the other boys by his remaining. No doubt there are those who in a case of doubt would always sacrifice the individual boy, and others who would never do so; but most people would agree that here there was a problem to be solved, and that it was not to be solved easily. So too with the work of the priest in the confessional; he has responsibilities towards God, towards the Church and towards the individual penitent; so he needs constantly to pray (in the words of the Whitsun collect) for a right judgement in all things. (See further ch. 7.)

It has been customary in the past to make a different analysis of the priest's work, and to say that in the confessional he acts as judge, as father, as physician, and as teacher. These are not watertight compartments, but it will be useful to consider each in turn.

I

JUDGE

The view is commonly expressed nowadays that the notion that the priest acts as a judge is entirely wrong. But this is only an extreme reaction against the excessively juridical way of approach which has been characteristic until recently of the Roman Catholic Church. There need be no atmosphere of law courts, of crimes, of penalties and punishments, for a priest to act as judge. Indeed, unless he exercises judgement, it is hard to see why the Lord gave his power to retain sins as well as to absolve them. Since there is the power to retain sins, it is clear that the priest needs to have the facts of the case before him—generalities are not enough—and to decide what decision is in accordance with the mind of his Master.

Rare though the occasions may be, it is necessary to consider when a priest should refuse to absolve.

(1) He should not absolve if the penitent has failed to confess any sins at all. This is not a common experience, but occasionally it might happen that the one 'sin' confessed was a failure to get to church on Sunday as a result of having a broken leg. Here there has been defective teaching; there is an obligation of Sunday worship, but it is binding on a man only when he is, e.g., physically able to go. In such a case the priest will gently explain the reason why it is not a sin, and will send the penitent away with a blessing. Alternatively, he will suggest that though the 'sin' turned out not to be sinful, yet there may well be small sins which the penitent has committed; in the case mentioned, the priest might well say, 'I expect that you have not always been patient or cheerful under your disability', and when the penitent agrees, he can give absolution. It is standard Roman Catholic practice for the penitent to be told to confess some sin of his past life, and for absolution then to be given, but this is artificial, to say the least.

(2) He should not absolve if the penitent has no sorrow for sin or purpose of amendment. In the ordinary way these good dispositions may be presupposed. In the Church of England there is no rule about the necessity of sacramental confession, and the fact that a penitent comes at all is *prima facie* testimony to his sincerity. Where sacramental confession is enforced or expected, there is great danger that someone may come only under compulsion and lacking any serious intentions. Since sorrow for sin and purpose of amendment are essential prerequisities, it would be wrong to absolve such a penitent. But it should rarely be necessary to dismiss anyone unabsolved.

A sulky boy in Holy Week might be disarmed by the priest starting like this: 'I expect you are only here because your parents pushed you into it?' When he readily and with surprise agrees, the priest might continue: 'You must get very tired of being nagged and pushed around. But all the same, you don't want to make yourself and other people unhappy by living that sort of selfish life; you do want to love and serve God better, don't you?' And little by little the right dispositions will be awakened. And a similar method can be used with depressed adults: 'I don't feel sorry about these things, father, and I'm sure I shall do them again.'

St Alphonsus wrote, 'How many penitents have come to me not disposed, and I have endeavoured with the help of divine grace to dispose them, and I have certainly done so, and, to my very great comfort, dismissed them with absolution.' This is a great pastoral opportunity, and a good-humoured and optimistic realism can rouse people to new hopefulness and effort.

The same thing applies if a penitent declares himself to be without faith. Disbelief would disqualify from absolution, but this may be seen to be a mood or passing feeling, or an awareness of intellectual difficulties. The penitent can be shown that he must have faith of some sort, or he would not be making his confession at all: surely he is relying on the Lord's promise, 'Him that cometh to me I will in no wise cast out'.

(3) What if the priest doubts the sincerity of the penitent because he knows him to have committed a grave sin which he fails to confess, even after discreet questioning? The standard books on confession often deal with this question at some length. All that needs to be said here is that such cases are rare, and that the confessor needs to be very sure indeed of his facts before refusing to believe the penitent, since even the most categorical statements of other people or the most obvious inferences may be mistaken. Also, unlikely as it may seem, the penitent may have forgotten, or he may be under the impression that the sin was not a serious one, or he may have confessed it already.

Should a priest defer absolution in some cases? In general very little good is done by delay, and there is danger of great harm. In theory, no doubt, the delay of a day or two may induce a greater sense of the seriousness of the sin and a firmer resolution to amend. But any priest who has heard a penitent say, 'Since my last confession forty-one years ago, when I was refused absolution, or rather, when it was deferred', is unwilling to risk such a result. Sometimes a penitent may be eager to put right a serious wrong which he has done and may wish to do that first to show his sincerity, and occasionally in a case of grave scandal this may be permitted. But it is wiser for the priest to give absolution at once and so to show that he trusts the penitent. He may have to insist on doing so, pointing out that the prodigal son was welcomed without question and invited at once to partake of a feast—he was not given a probationary period on bread and water to make sure that he really was rightly disposed. Reluctance to give absolution may seem to imply a grudging attitude on the part of God towards the sinner.

What about conditional absolution? The objections to deferring absolution apply also to conditional absolution in many cases. One can imagine cases when it is justified, e.g., if the confessor is uncertain whether the penitent is baptized, or if it is discovered, perhaps at the end of a confession, that the penitent is, say, a Methodist or a member of the Swedish Church, and one is uncertain about one's *locus standi*. One can insert a condition, 'If I have the authority to do so'. It would be quite wrong to make as a condition something future ('if you give up this sin'; 'if you say your prayers for the next week'). The confessor cannot be certain that the penitent will still be alive.

It is unnecessary to deal with the question of reserved cases, i.e. grave sins which a diocesan bishop reserves to himself or his special delegates for treatment, since the Church of England does not in fact withdraw any sins from absolution by an ordinary confessor. It would appear that even in the Roman Catholic Church, where there is an elaborate system of reservation, the abundance of exceptions defeats any purpose the system may have. Were excommunication to be revived as a spiritual penalty, it would be necessary for the same or equivalent authority to remove the penalty as originally imposed it—in other words it would not be within the competence of an ordinary parish priest to absolve or admit to communion.[1]

The zealous confessor must be careful not to create difficulties for himself and his penitent or to disturb his penitent's conscience unnecessarily. He seeks to train his penitent and to teach him progressively; is he obliged to point out difficulties which his penitent has not noticed, or examine him about duties which, if pointed out, the penitent would probably fail to undertake? In general, no. It is a mistake to create difficulties; and if a penitent in good faith is probably failing in a department of Christian duty, it is usually better not to raise the matter in question. As his conscience becomes more sensitive, he may do so himself, and this is much to be preferred.

[1] For the case of a bishop in the Roman Catholic Church who in the nineteenth century reserved to himself a great many sins (including drunkenness and all forms of dancing) with lamentable results to his people, see J. M. T. Barton, *Penance and Absolution*, p. 76, footnote 10. Cf. also p. 85 below.

Otherwise there is grave danger of too great a burden being placed on
weak shoulders.

Akin to this is the question of hypothetical sins which plague some
penitents. 'I am very lacking in faith and love, because I am sure that
if certain things happened and a choice were demanded of me, I
should never have the courage to choose rightly.' Such a person may
be encouraged to confess defective faith and love, but he must also
be told not to be concerned with the future. God does not provide
us with larger quantities of courage and other virtues long before the
need to exhibit them. It is when the crisis comes that it is time to look
to God for strength, and one does not look in vain. But a Christian
can get hopelessly discouraged and despairing just because he cannot
be sure that he would not under torture renounce his God. He must
be told to pay attention to the existing circumstances of his life and
to follow Christ and embrace his cross in them; the future can look
after itself. It is right to be unsure of one's perseverance; but the best
way to prepare for faithfulness under extreme temptation is to be
faithful to the Saviour under one's existing temptations. So when
the neurotic penitent almost asks not to be absolved because of this
hypothetical lack of determination in possible future circumstances,
he must be told to concentrate his attention on the present and not
to agitate himself foolishly and unnecessarily.

II
FATHER

It is customary for the penitent to address his confessor as 'Father',
though to omit to do so would not cause surprise—it would be
unlikely to be noticed. Whether or not the priest who hears a
confession is called Father, he certainly needs to show a father's
understanding and love. But what sort of father is he to imitate? The
heavy Victorian father, whose word was law and at whose frown
everyone trembled? Or the contemporary American father, who,
it is said, has abdicated responsibility as much as possible, and is
prepared to gang up with his children against the seat of authority
(represented by his wife)?

It is a matter of great importance that this should be cleared up,
since one has much sympathy with the arguments which are urged
against the practice of sacramental confession—if the facts were

really what they are sometimes thought to be, the author of this book also would be against it. John Stott speaks of the

> danger of clergy tying people to their apron strings, instead of encouraging them to develop a certain sturdy and healthy independence, as they rely more and more upon God himself. It was surely to this that Jesus referred when he warned us to call no man our 'father', 'teacher' or 'lord' on earth (Matt. 23.8-12). We are to adopt towards no one in the church, nor require anyone to adopt towards us, the dependent attitude implied in the child-parent, pupil–teacher, servant–lord relationships. We are all brethren. We are to depend on God as our Father, Christ as our Lord, and the Holy Spirit as our Teacher. The ambition of every minister for his congregation should be so to warn every man in all wisdom as to 'present every man' not dependent on his minister but 'full-grown, mature in Christ' (Col. 1.28).[2]

This is splendidly said and wins the assent of all who are called to hear confessions. The confessor does not wish to perpetuate the Victorian father without whose permission nothing might be done. Very forcefully Mgr Gay refused such a role in a letter to a penitent who wanted to receive commands:

> Such commands would relieve you of the burdens of life, but it is not good that you should not feel the weight of them. I will be to you as the Cyrenian, nothing more. I would help you, not substitute myself for you.... I do not want you to be a slave—the word is your own—a word excessive and reprehensible. I wish you to be a son, and a son reasonable, enlightened by the counsels of his father ... but walking as a man, not as a child.[3]

A priest is delighted and not dismayed when a penitent whom he has been trying to help over many months and who has always been responsive and co-operative, firmly but politely expresses a different point of view and decides to follow another path than the one tentatively suggested.

How then has this erroneous idea arisen? Because tradition dies hard in the Church, and because, in the days of Victorian fathers, priests tended to make their fatherhood agree with the normal

---

[2] *Confess Your Sins*, p. 82.
[3] *Lettres de Direction Spirituelle*, IV. 10, quoted in Bede Frost, *The Art of Mental Prayer* (SPCK 1940), pp. 214-15.

pattern, and this regrettably lives on in some quarters. Add to this the Irish influence in the Roman Catholic Church—the Irish priest in the past has exercised a degree of influence over the lives of his flock which was excessive. If there is no one but yourself to lead and direct a backward and ignorant community, then it is hard, whether you are Catholic, Protestant, or nothing at all, to refrain from a paternalism which however well intentioned and fruitful of good in the short run, is in the long run enfeebling and disastrous. The loyalty which will entertain no criticism of the priest or of the Pope has a fine side to it, but collegiality and co-responsibility are fine ideas too, and an open-eyed loyalty is much to be preferred to a blind and unquestioning one. No confessor worth his salt takes the attitude 'Theirs not to reason why'. The penitent *should* reason why; only very rarely should the confessor decline to give reasons or expect implicit obedience.[4] For he should always be aiming to do himself out of a job. He desires that his people should cease to commit sin and that they should be wholly responsive to the guidance of the Holy Spirit. But as long as sin injures their souls and distorts their understandings, his fatherly care will be required.

To be fatherly without being paternalist—that is the confessor's aim. But there are some in every congregation who wish to be spoonfed; they do not wish to think for themselves, they wish to be told what to do. (These are just as likely to become dependent upon a preacher as on a confessor.) In the confessional the wise priest will not answer their questions yes or no. 'Tell me whether I should go to that dance, should I resign from this society, should I apply to enter that college?' The priest will often throw the question back: 'What do *you* think God wants you to do?' 'What makes you say that?' 'Aren't there two aspects which you have to weigh one against the other, these?' In this manner he can elucidate the points at issue and deter the penitent from coming to even the right conclusion from the wrong motive or through fallacious reasoning.

A simple penitent, for example, might well argue that since the first and great commandment is to love God with one's whole being, and the second is to love one's neighbour, a religious duty such as going to Bible class or receiving one's communion should always take precedence of visiting a lonely friend. It would be the reverse of helpful to be told, 'Go and see your friend!'—particularly if this

[4] See pp. 86-90 on the treatment of scrupulous penitents.

were said in a brusque way, as if to imply that only a fool would think otherwise. The right path may indeed be obvious to the confessor, but he should not just supply the right conclusion, but show the penitent how that conclusion was reached; or, better still, enable the penitent to reach that conclusion for himself. The priest will hold up the supreme example of Lord Jesus: 'Do you remember the story Jesus told about the donkey that fell into a pit on the sabbath day? Some of his hearers thought that the duty of honouring God by not doing anything that could be called work on the sabbath took precedence of every other consideration. Why do you think Jesus took the opposite point of view?' In this sort of way the priest encourages the penitent to look for the answer to his uncertainties in Jesus and to be obedient not to his confessor but to the Spirit of Jesus who enlightens his understanding.

All this will be done by the priest as a fellow disciple and fellow student of the Scriptures. He will not lose patience with the woman who has to be told again and again to look to Jesus himself for the answers, or with the man who always uses the same glib formula to solve all problems. Schoolchildren hate teachers who employ sarcasm in dealing with them, and the sarcastic priest quickly drives people away who are in need of help. Almost equally dangerous is smartness of repartee and a taste for epigram; the desire to score off one's penitent, in however good a cause, must be quickly quenched. 'He must increase, I must decrease' was John the Baptist's aim in relation to Jesus; and it is better to instil the words of Jesus than epigrams of one's own devising.

Gentleness was a characteristic of Jesus, and the confessor shows a father's gentleness. 'Like as a father pitieth his own children, even so is the Lord merciful unto them that fear him' (Ps. 103.13). It is this that most surprises the person who has plucked up courage to make his first confession. His sins seem so burdensome to him, they are so horrible, they have been so wilful, that he fully expects to receive a fearful dressing-down from the man who represents God himself; it will be just what he deserves, so he is prepared for a terrible ordeal. But that is just what he does not receive. Instead of being lashed with reproaches as he expects and deserves, it is rather the welcome which the prodigal son received. It is not that the sin itself is being condoned, far from it; but God's instantaneous acceptance of the penitent sinner is communicated, and this generosity is far more painful and affecting that any number of reproaches. To be kissed when you deserve to be cursed—it is this that almost breaks the prodigal's heart and immeasurably strengthens his newly found resolve to amend his ways. The story would have had a very different ending if the first person the prodigal had come across had been his elder brother. No doubt a gentle person can also be tough at times, but it is sad when it is toughness that is thought to be characteristic of a priest. Sometimes one who has lapsed for years shrinks from making his confession, fearing that he will be bitterly reproached: and one knows that there are a few priests who would imitate the prodigal's elder brother. Yet nothing could be more ruinous. Even if the prodigal's father has a shrewd suspicion that his newly restored son will not be content with the fatted calf but will expect breakfast in bed the next day, nonetheless the fatted calf should still be killed, and it will be soon enough next day to show that both sons are expected to get up at dawn to go about their daily tasks.

Closely allied to gentleness is patience. Izaak Walton observed that 'it is some relief for a poor body to be but heard with patience'. It is usually wise to allow the penitent to recount his sins in his own way. It may be full of irrelevances, but no matter; it may be woefully inadequate, but some of the inadequacies can be remedied later on. At all costs the priest must restrain himself; he must not fidget, yawn, or take a surreptitious look at his watch—all this is fatal to the penitent's confidence in him. If the priest's meal-time is imperilled, let the priest remember that his Master too sometimes had not the leisure to eat. So he will not interrupt without the best of reasons; and never will he show the slightest disgust or surprise or curiosity.

Why should it be wrong to interject, 'Oh, how terrible!' it may be asked. Surely that would quietly underline the seriousness of the sin confessed? Agreed. But there is no need to do any such thing. Of course the thing is terrible, otherwise the penitent would not be kneeling there. He will not mistake silence for condonation. Keep silent; otherwise if you express concern or dismay, the penitent may not dare to confess the greater sin which comes next. He will argue that if his confessor is moved to show such concern about lesser sins, he would be immeasurably shocked by further disclosures, and therefore it would be preferable to hide them. Thus the confessor will have caused serious damage by making the penitent conceal some of his sins.

It is scarcely possible to stress the importance of this too much.

With a first confession especially there is liable to be uncertainty and embarrassment, and nothing should be taken for granted. It is so much easier to come clean, if one's confessor is matter-of-fact and un-emotional—in a word, if he is professional. The patient in a hospital loses his fears in proportion as he sees that he is being treated not by amateurs but by professionals, and in so far as he sees that their concern is to cure him, not to pass condemnatory judgements on his physical state and how he came to be in it. A priest can and should inspire the same sort of confidence, and here the analogy with the doctor is a good one. For a doctor, besides being professional, is a human being. Though he treats his patient professionally, he does not go about his work with inhuman detachment, as though the patient were only an interesting case, and as though he were not in any way interested in him as a person. So too the priest, while show-ing professional calm and expertise, will take care not to be merely slick, doling out the appropriate advice or remedies but in an inhuman and clinical way.

The ideal father has no favourites in the family—or rather, what-ever his instinctive preferences, he exhibits no favouritism towards the various members of the family. Similarly the priest in the con-fessional shows a father's love to all. He takes care not even to think in terms like 'only a child's confession' or 'only another holy woman' or 'this awful man'. Each person who kneels beside him is someone for whom the Saviour Jesus Christ died, someone for whom the Father has an infinite love and concern. Unattractive—to say no more—as the individual may be, that is neither here nor there: he is dear to God, and he needs to have God's love and care mediated to him. It must make no difference if he stammers, if he is long-winded, if he is half-witted, if he is neurotic, if he is late for the appointment —Christ's courtesy never comes amiss, and it has a healing influence of the greatest value. How apt is the comment of St Francis of Sales, that you catch more flies with a spoonful of honey than with a gallon of vinegar! People are easily discouraged, and they readily sense it if they are unwelcome. On the other hand, they are never afraid to return if they know that they will not be upbraided and that nothing is too much trouble for their confessor.

The worse the sins which are confessed, the more the priest will rejoice that the sinner has been able to confess them and that he himself is privileged to bring the necessary healing to the sick and wounded person. Like the surgeon who performs an emergency operation, he is thankful to be in a position to save a soul from death. But though such an experience makes him vividly aware how worthwhile a job he performs, he does not feel it beneath his dignity to take great trouble with the lesser ailments which others bring to him; he will never make those who only confess small sins feel unwanted or undeserving of his attention. If ever he finds himself impatient of confessions of devotion, he should consider whether he himself is pressing on still towards perfection. For it is human nature to resent the example of those who are trying harder than oneself.

In spite of what has been said, the confessor will never take sin for granted in the sense that he accepts it as inevitable and unimportant. Love and concern for the sinner will never make him see sin as anything but ugly and monstrous, a blot on God's creation. So he will show the penitent that it is fearful ingratitude to turn one's back on God; the New Testament even describes apostasy as a crucifying and mocking of the Son of God (Heb. 6.6). But this should be mentioned only in order to highlight the glory of God's forgiveness; 'He hath not dealt with us after our sins, nor rewarded us according to our wickedness' (Ps. 103.10). It is not for nothing that the penitent usually kneels with a crucifix before his eyes. It is from Jesus that he looks for pardon, since 'he is the sacrifice that takes our sins away' (1 John 2.2), and the price of the sinner's reconciliation with God was Calvary's cross. To look at the figure of the Crucified is to see the havoc wrought by sin together with the astonishing love of God.

Because of this miracle of God's love the confessor will never fail to be encouraging. 'With God on our side who can be against us?' (Rom. 8.13): there can never be any place for despair. The more penitent the sinner, the less forgivable he will think himself to be; and the priest must firmly insist that God is infinitely forgiving, that there is no 'thus far and no further' with him. Like Paul, the priest will affirm: 'I am quite certain that the One who began this good work in you will see that it is finished when the Day of Christ Jesus comes' (Phil. 1.6).

The grievous sinner may find it hard to believe that all is forgiven, and he will find comfort and strength in the unequivocal words of absolution: *By his authority ... I absolve thee from all thy sins.* But the priest soon learns that there is no one who does not welcome a word of encouragement, the faithful and conscientious Christian no less than the apparently lukewarm. Weariness and disillusionment beset most people from time to time; a few are hardly ever free of them; on some keen people they descend suddenly with disconcerting severity. According to one account, Jesus told the paralysed man not only, 'Your sins are forgiven', but also, 'Courage, my child'— 'be of good cheer' (Matt. 9.2). The greatest saint no less than the worst sinner requires this fatherly encouragement; and the least experienced confessor, even if gems of spirituality do not drop readily from his lips, can send the penitent sinner away rejoicing and full of the assurance that the struggle is infinitely worth while.

Give a dog a bad name, and hang him. It would be fatal to treat someone as hopeless—he would justify your lack of trust. But expect big things of them, and often you will not be disappointed. Queen Elizabeth I is said to have made men trustworthy by trusting them; and this is precisely what a priest should do in the confessional. He will be always full of hope, not because he thinks that everyone is good at heart, but because he knows that God is full of power and love. The soap opera shows the big bad man melting when a tiny child appeals to him—to think that he of all people should be trusted ! The Victorian painting of the burglar and the little girl pointed the same moral, 'Will 'oo mend my dolly?' But there is truth under these layers of sentimentality. Of course this approach does not always 'work'—did Jesus convert everyone he met? But this is the way of love, and the most fruitful pastoral method.

Just because the priest is to emulate a father, is he therefore never to be stern? Just because he is a father, he will occasionally be stern. He may detect a note of levity in what a penitent says; in this case he will remind him that he is making his confession to God and at the foot of the cross of Jesus Christ: he is not pouring out confidences to a barman. But even so an indirect method of rebuke is to be preferred. 'You are telling God that you are sorry for your sins, aren't you? You are trying to look at them seriously and objectively, since such selfishness does so much harm, and so displeases Jesus.' Ascribe the right attitude to the penitent, and even if he hitherto lacked it, he will try to adopt it. It is wiser to be too mild with someone who is hardened than too sharp with someone who is embarrassed. Embarrassment may make a penitent giggle or seem offhand and uncommunicative; so the confessor will be slow to rebuke or accuse. And if a reprimand has to be given, it can be followed at once by words which show a loving confidence that it will be understood and acted upon.

Though the seal of confession is absolute, it is unwise for a priest to hear the confessions of his own relatives, close friends, or employees. Sometimes this may be unavoidable, and no absolute rule should be made. But such relationships may readily lead to the penitent making inadequate confessions, suppressing sins because of the consequent shame or distress. As will be explained in the chapter on the seal of confession, the confessor will under no circumstances make use of any information obtained in the confessional. He will not dismiss a dishonest servant or in any way alter his attitude towards a promiscuous colleague or drug-addicted son— nor should he on the basis of information *not* received withdraw a servant's dismissal or behave differently from normal.

Most of the confessor's difficulties are solved in advance if he himself has been in the habit of making his confession to an experienced priest. He will then know by experience what a difference simple courtesy and kindliness make in administration of this sacramental means of grace, how greatly one can be helped by the simplest words of advice and encouragement, and how off-putting a cold formalism can be (if on the odd occasion he has been unlucky in his choice of a priest).

III

PHYSICIAN

Health or wholeness was the objective of Jesus in relation to all those who came to him in distress. His cures were bodily, mental, and spiritual, to use a convenient if question-begging classification. For whatever usefulness there may be in having body specialists, mind specialists and spirit specialists (and the usefulness cannot be disputed), it is increasingly seen nowadays that a human being is a unity, and that he himself is the object of the cure, rather than just a part of himself.

Specialist though he is, the priest is the representative of the Saviour who was and is concerned with every part of man's being. He speaks of the God who created the world, and not simply of the God of redemption and sanctification. Like the character in the play of Terence, every priest should be able to affirm, 'I am a man; I count nothing human indifferent to me'. So, though it is not his immediate concern, he is involved in the physical and mental welfare of his people, and will never speak slightingly of those whose ministry of healing is focused more particularly on those aspects. To think only of people's souls is to encourage belief in a Sundays-only God, a God who (in the narrow sense of the word) is concerned only with religion. But such a peripheral God is not the Christian God at all; he is the God tolerated by totalitarian systems of society because he causes no trouble; such a private God is as harmless as a pet colour or lucky number.

Healing is one and indivisible, and all sections of it intercommunicate. So it is a common experience that a medical cure effects a spiritual revolution, and a spiritual revolution effects a medical cure. One would be happier with the claim of the enthusiast that 'the doctors and psychiatrists had given me up as hopeless, and prayer cured me' and with the publicity which church magazines give to it, if the same people were prepared to publicize the equally well attested cases of those who prayed and prayed without getting anywhere, only to have their spiritual problems resolved by medical or psychiatric means. There is no need for anyone to be jealous, since all healing redounds to the glory of God.

In earlier days priests might trespass on the province of the doctor without blame. John Wesley wrote a book about physical complaints and diseases and the appropriate remedies; but the priest who did this nowadays would be suspect among the medical practitioners of his parish. There is little danger today of priest and doctor interfering with each other's work. But the relationship between priest and psychiatrist is not such an easy one; it will be considered at greater length in ch. 7.

The growth of modern psychology has, however, greatly assisted the priest in his ministrations. It has almost abolished the bitter prejudice against the confessional which was common in the last century, when it occupied hours of parliamentary time and excited widespread hostility. It is now fully accepted that detailed and lengthy conversations on sexual and kindred subjects will take place in the psychiatrist's consulting room, and it is no longer thought indelicate for such matters to be discussed with a priest. The man in the street may not be aware of the different methods employed by psychiatrist and priest, but he is not horrified at the mention of sex in the way that most of his Victorian forebears were. Both priest and psychiatrist are likely to be the recipients of confidences, and quite apart from absolution or therapy there are not a few who benefit from a consultation with the one or the other.

Both may sometimes have to give advice, but that is not the precise job of either of them. Each in his own way seeks to work on a deeper level of healing. Love is the agent of healing, whether it is the total acceptance of his patient, both the good side and the bad side, by the psychiatrist, or the total acceptance of the penitent by the priest in the name of the all-loving Saviour. Neither is an easygoing love, for there is that in men which shrinks from being healed if it means a total opening out, whether to the inexorable and patient questioning of the psychiatrist, or to the relentless quest of the Hound of Heaven. For it is above all else faith which the priest seeks to evoke—he is not interested in mere improvement. Faith in God opens a man's being to infinite possibilities, and whoever is in need of healing must be led constantly into the presence of Jesus: his words and his sacraments are irradiated by the love of the Almighty Father.

One of the most important of healing truths is the distinction between temptation and sin. This should be obvious to anyone, but it is not. How often people are in despair not so much about their sins as about their temptations! 'If I were the right sort of person, if I were a true Christian, if I had given myself to Christ, these awful desires would not obsess me'—so they argue. Often these obsessive temptations are sexual—a man wants to seduce young children; or he lusts after members of his own sex; he wants to expose himself to women. There may be other factors: he sometimes has a violent temptation to kill someone who is dear to him: he would willingly torture an animal or a child. Or blasphemy may come in: at the holiest moments of worship he may picture everything being defiled, and awareness of God only seems to provoke the desire to utter filthy blasphemies. The first step in helping such a person is to show that temptation is one thing and sin another, and that the temptations might be a hundred times more shocking, and still there would be no sin. He must think of himself as resembling a man trying to listen to a concert and having the misfortune to endure a pneumatic drill just outside the window. It is undeniably tiresome, but it is not his fault.

Secondly, the nuisance value of the obsession is much reduced if it is faced clinically instead of being feared. They are caused in all probability by something so odd that if one ever discovered the cause, one could have a good laugh about it, for we are strange beings. Instead of hoping against hope that these wretched thoughts won't reappear, the penitent will be encouraged to *expect* them without getting horrified or upset. 'Here we go again !' should be the reaction, rather than panic—and rather than frenzied prayers. If the person is to pray, his prayers should not be merely negative, addressed *against* the threatening danger. They should be positive acts of faith and trust. Best of all are firm statements like 'The Lord is my light and my salvation : whom then shall I fear? The Lord is the strength of my life : of whom then shall I be afraid?' (Ps. 27.1).

'Is it a mortal sin or a venial sin?' is a question which may be put to the confessor especially by a penitent who has imbibed the Roman Catholic approach to confession. For the teaching of the Council of Trent was that sacramental confession was necessary for salvation in the case of those who had committed mortal sin after baptism. To be in good standing it is necessary as a matter of discipline to make one's confession sincerely once a year, if one has committed mortal sins, as also before receiving Holy Communion. Some modern Roman Catholic writers believe that it is a matter of ecclesiastical law, and not of divine law, that Communion after unconfessed mortal sin is forbidden.[5] Since there is no such obligation in the Church of England, it is not a matter of such urgency to determine which are mortal and which venial sins. But for a variety of reasons it is almost equally necessary to examine the matter.

It may be thought dangerous and undesirable to make any distinction between mortal and venial, big or little, sins. Is not all sin a grievous offence against God, and does it not encourage laxity to speak of a venial sin—with the implication that it is *only* a venial sin? This is true, and there were not a few Anglican theologians in the seventeenth century who expressed themselves strongly on the subject. But granted that it is dangerous, what is the alternative? To regard all sins as equal? To feel as totally unworthy to receive Holy Communion after swearing at falling down the stairs as after committing murder or adultery? It may be attractive to the eager seeker after Christian perfection to regard all sins as alike and therefore equally mortal; but the ordinary run-of-the-road Christian ultimately would find that absurd, the earnest Christian ultimately would find it intolerable, and the end result would be that all sins without exception would be regarded as venial. No. There is plenty of good precedent for being discriminating: Hebrews seems to regard

[5] See the footnote to p. 45 of *Penance: Virtue and Sacrament*, ed. Fitzsimons, and article there quoted.

some sins as unforgivable (6.4-6) and others therefore forgivable;
John distinguishes a 'sin unto death' from a 'sin not unto death'
(1 John 5.16-17), and this is in line with the teaching of Jesus himself
who distinguished between those who knowingly did things worthy
of stripes and those who did the same unknowingly (Luke 12.47-8).
Charles Williams summed the matter up in some memorable words:

> In morals, as in everything, there are two opposite tendencies.
> The first is to say: 'Everything matters infinitely.' The second is
> to say: 'No doubt that is true. But mere sanity demands that we
> should not treat everything as mattering all that. Distinction is
> necessary; more-or-less is necessary; indifference is necessary.' The
> contention is always sharp. The Rigorous view is vital to sanctity;
> the Relaxed view is vital to sanity. Their union is not impossible,
> but it is difficult; for whichever is in power begins, after the first
> five minutes, to maintain itself from bad and unworthy motives.
> Harshness, pride, resentment encourage the one; indulgence, falsity,
> detestable good-fellowship the other (*The Descent of the Dove*,
> p. 31).

As chapter 2 has shown, there was a strong inclination in the early
Church to regard apostasy, murder, and adultery as sins which could
not be forgiven in this life. But as circumstances changed, milder
counsels prevailed, and even those who had committed such grave
sins as these were reconciled. Augustine, with his profound knowledge of the human heart, fully recognized the difference between
bigger and lesser sins, but could also write: 'What those sins are
which exclude from the kingdom of God, it is most difficult to
determine and most dangerous to assign.' He distinguished three
classes of sins: first, those involving excommunication and public
penance; next, those that need to be taken seriously and corrected
by sharp reproof; and lastly, the everyday trivial failures. This is a
common-sense classification, and made sense in the fifth century
when he wrote, before the excessively juridical and penal aspect of
penance became dominant.

When private confession superseded public penance, there came
to be regular tariffs of penances for sins, the penance being regarded
as the penalty incurred. A penance might last for ten years or only
for twenty-four hours, depending on the gravity of the sin. Thus
Augustine's first and second classes of sins merged, leaving only
trivial sins outside. Thus the scope of mortal sins was much widened,

and came to include anything at all serious; and in practice this has tended to be the Roman Catholic attitude until recently. It is hardly too much to say that to be in so-called mortal sin was the normal state of the average believer, from which only priestly absolution could release you. (It is true that an act of perfect contrition would do so, but as this had to be accompanied by a resolve to seek priestly absolution, this scarcely made an exception.) This could lead to ludicrous results: eating more than a small quantity of meat on a Friday, unless there were mitigating circumstances, was mortal sin.

Such strictness was self-defeating. It seemed to be a God very different from the Father of our Lord Jesus Christ who might consign a devout Catholic to hell for having strayed from the right path to this small extent and having failed to follow it up with an act of contrition or by confession. A healthier and more robust opinion is growing up which sees mortal sin as something which it is *difficult* for a conscientious Christian to commit—it is not something which he will often, almost to his surprise, find himself committing. It is simply untrue that many of these allegedly mortal sins at once inflict a death wound on the soul. They may be grave, they may be highly blameworthy, but, as has often been pointed out, the most that they can be called is *mortiferous*: their effect is serious though hardly 'deadly'. It seems as though some different classification is called for.

The less the penitent thinks in terms of mortal and venial sin, the better. For according to his temperament, he will either persuade himself that all his venial sins are mortal, which is the road to despair, or that all his mortal sins are venial, which is the road to presumption. Let the confessor decline to be drawn on this distinction, and instead insist on the gravity of all sin which pulls a child away from his heavenly Father. But the distinction is a useful one for the priest himself, for he is like a doctor called upon to treat someone with multiple injuries; he must swiftly decide which are the most serious and attend to them, while leaving the less serious to a later and more appropriate time. It is no time to worry about teeth knocked out when a man has a cut artery.

The confessor must not get preoccupied with sin, as though this should be his prime study, and he must not allow his penitent to become preoccupied with it. For the life of the Christian is not satisfactorily defined as one without sin—that would be like describing a beautiful fabric as being one without holes. The three theological

virtues, faith, hope, and love, must be his constant study; and
following them the four cardinal virtues, justice, temperance, for-
titude, and prudence. So he will be able to translate what are
described to him as sins and understand them as failures to achieve
virtues; and he will constantly be drawing the penitent's attention to
the loveliness of virtue, rather than dwelling on the ugliness of vice.
If the penitent should seem concerned about the commission of the
'seven deadly sins'[*] then he will always bring before his mind and
the mind of the penitent the virtues directly opposed to them.

How wise was Paul in telling his Philippian converts: 'Fill your
minds with everything that is true, everything that is noble, everything that is good and pure, everything that we love and honour,
and everything that can be thought virtuous or worthy of praise'
(Phil. 4.8)! The confessor will often have occasion to warn people
against such negative prayers as 'Don't let me lose my temper' and
'Don't let me give way to masturbation'. For the imagination is very
powerful, and the tempting image of sin, even when projected in
prayer to defeat it, is usually enough to sway the weakness of the
human will. It is far more effective to dwell on the Lord's presence
within one, to rejoice that he has brought all his lovely virtues with
him, and to bear in mind that opportunities to display them all will
be forthcoming, and not only so but also that the power to exercise
them is within. Rather than pray desperately, 'Give me strength not
to lose my temper', it is better to say, 'Thank you for bringing me
your own patience and love'.

There is much to criticize in Christian Science, but Christians can
learn something from the techniques of its practitioners.

The therapy employed in (Christian) Science consists of finding
out what belongs to the patient's true and genuine God-given
nature. Science stresses what is divinely right with him, not what
is wrong. Thus the Scientist strives to bring to light the integrity,
strength, purity, goodness and perfection of man's real individuality
as the reflection of God (De Witt John, *The Christian Science Way
of Life*, p. 180).

[*] A misnomer, since they may or may not be deadly: certainly they are
'capital', being that from which all other sins spring; they represent misdirected
instinctive energy.

IV
GUIDE

The priest is the person who has specialized in his subject; he is therefore able to teach and direct the penitent who comes to him for help in living the Christian life. But as teacher he does not set himself up as infallible, and as director he does not demand implicit obedience. For if he is teacher and director, he is also fellow disciple and fellow sinner, so he does not speak *de haut en bas*. Like the best teachers of today, he prefers not to instruct by handing out pellets of information or recipes to be followed without question; rather he puts the person he is seeking to instruct in the way of discovering the truth for himself.

The confessor does well to ponder some words of Frederick William Faber: 'He does not lead his penitents; the Holy Ghost leads them. He holds out his hands from behind, as a mother does to her tottering child, to balance his uncertain steps as he sways overmuch, now on one side, now on another.' As director he does not stand in the position of theosophical adept, issuing instructions which, though unverifiable, must be followed implicitly. He has the minor but important task of helping the penitent to follow the directions which the Holy Spirit is communicating to his conscience. So he firmly discourages any attempt on the part of his penitent to make him the supreme arbiter.

He needs above all things to be supernaturally minded himself, to be full of hunger and thirst after righteousness, to live with his heart in heaven, and so be able to fire others with the same devotion. 'He must make them see the personal nature of religion, personal love, devotion and service for God in Jesus Christ; not a mere tame acquiescence in a moral code, but a burning enthusiasm for a Master, a passion of the lover for the beloved'.[7]

And the same author says: 'Too much direction is moral rather than spiritual, more concerned with sin than with God, with self-examination and self-improvement rather than with the search for God.[8]

Much the same point is made in more psychological terms by Harry Williams in his essay in *Soundings* (p. 90).

[7] Frost, op. cit., p. 225.
[8] Ibid., p. 219.

The opposite of sin can only be faith and can never be virtue. When I attempt to make myself virtuous, the me I can thus organize and discipline is no more than the me of which I am aware. And it is precisely the equation of my total self with this one small part of it which is the root cause of all sin. This is the fundamental mistake often made in exhortations to repentance and amendment. They attempt to confirm me in my lack of faith by getting me to organize the self I know against the self I do not know.... Faith on the other hand consists in the awareness that I am more than I know.

The priest must always be the preacher of salvation not of improvement.

A useful distinction is made by Martin Thornton in his *Pastoral Theology: A Reorientation* (p. 8) between teaching and coaching; he shows that spiritual direction should be envisaged in terms of the latter.

Strictly, to teach cricket means to give classroom instruction on the rules, strategy, and possibly moral implications of the game, while coaching is the practical development of technique and correction of faults in matches and net-practice.... 'Teaching the faith', then, is a contradiction : only belief can be taught, whereas faith arises and deepens through direction.

And in *Christian Proficiency*, a book which it is difficult to praise too highly, he explains what he means at greater length. Here is an essentially traditionalist approach to spiritual direction which is not bemused by stock answers but attempts to rethink principles sanely in the contemporary situation. The author expresses himself pungently and sometimes defiantly; it is profitable reading for the conservative, who will term it radical, and for the radical, who will call it conservative.

On the rule of life, or Rule, as he prefers to call it, he writes things which every confessor should read. For many penitents are in the habit of confessing as sins what are in fact only breaches of rule. He rightly insists that failure to keep one's rule does not constitute sin; there may indeed have been a sin which caused the breach of the rule (being too drunk to pray, or too lazy to get up), but *in itself* to breach the rule is morally indifferent. The *sin* is the drunkenness or the laziness. In certain circumstances it will be virtuous to breach the rule (missing one's communion in order to rescue someone from danger).* The spiritual director may well bear in the mind the words of the late Father W. B. O'Brien, S.S.J.E.: 'We spend one half of our life learning to keep a rule, and the other half learning how it has to be broken to accommodate ourselves to life.'

Experience has shown that the spiritual life divides into three parts, the purgative way, the illuminative way, and the unitive way. No one has ever claimed that this classification is more than a rough and ready guide, and it is a mistake to think of three distinct sections of a road with quite different characteristics and scenery. Perhaps learning to swim is a more apposite illustration. At first the would-be swimmer remains at the shallow end of the swimming pool or close to the shore of the sea; he needs elementary instruction in the correct strokes and for the avoiding of obvious mistakes. If he is over-confident, he soon gets into difficulties and panics, and there is a good deal of spluttering and alarm. Yet even he has his moments when he feels master of this new element and seems at home in the water.

As time goes on, he more and more stays out of his depth at the deep end of the pool or beyond the breakers in the sea. Here he will learn superior techniques and greater speed. Sometimes these will enable him to venture much further from the shore; sometimes he will need to return to the shallows, but less and less often.

He reaches perfection as a swimmer when he is wholly at home in the sea, when swimming seems as natural as breathing, and when even swimming the English Channel is not daunting, exhausting as it may be. Now it is unthinkable that he should not be disporting himself in the water—it is the most natural thing in the world.

There are many other ways of expressing the same thing. After the disciples had been with Jesus for some time, he was able to say to them, 'I shall not call you servants any more, because a servant does not know his master's business; I call you friends, because I have made known to you everything I have learnt from my Father' (John 15.15). They no longer merely adhered to an external standard: that standard had been internalized, and they know from within themselves what the Father's will was. In such a state of 'illumination' the believer no longer asks how much is compulsory for him to do but rather how much he is permitted to do; he desires to give as much as possible rather than as little as possible.

Yet even this is not the summit. It is far more to be a friend of

* See the same author's *Prayer: A New Encounter* (1972) for further development of his views.

Jesus than merely to serve him, but there is a closer union still. Here the least unsatisfactory metaphor is that of marriage: 'My beloved is mine and I am his' (Song of Solomon 2.16). The believer is inter-penetrated by his Saviour; Christ is immanent in the soul rather than external to it. For it is no longer the Christian standards that have become part of the believer, it is Christ himself.

Just as there are many people who declare themselves to be 'schizophrenic' about something, when they mean something far less serious, so there are many penitents who have picked up technical terms from some spiritual writing and who diagnose themselves as being 'in the dark night of the soul'. The confessor must not be misled by this, for what they really mean is that they are bored with their prayers for one reason or another and are suffering from aridity. Even this aridity may be due not so much to an inability to pray as to the fact that they are compelling themselves to maintain an in-appropriate pattern of prayer or are burdened with tedious inter-cession lists sent to them by religious societies to which they belong. This does not mean that there is no such thing as the dark night of the soul, but only that, like schizophrenia, it is not such a common condition as some people's words might suggest.

However, whether in the dark night of the soul or in earlier stages, the director's wise encouragement can be of immense value to the perplexed and becalmed believer. It is a common and almost universal experience that prayers, meditations, and communions which in the past have brought joy and happiness, later seem lifeless and meaning-less. This can be a devastating trial even when one is expecting it, but to many disciples it comes as a totally unexpected desolation, proving to them, so they think, that all has been in vain and showing them either the unreality of God or the unreality of their previous devotion.

Yet, as spiritual writers are unanimous in affirming, this is a necessary stage in the progress of the disciple. Delight in God and in communion with him is indeed a foretaste of heaven, but such delight has to be rationed to us during our life, since otherwise we shall tend to be preoccupied less with God than with the delight which he gives. So painfully it is necessary to learn to love and serve him without delight. St Francis of Sales puts it thus:

God ordinarily gives a foretaste of heavenly delights to those who enter on his service, in order to withdraw them from earthly pleasures and encourage them in the pursuit of divine love, like a mother who, to entice and allure her little child to the breast, puts honey upon the end of the teat. It is nevertheless this good God who sometimes, according to the wise disposition of his providence, takes away from us the milk and honey of consolations, in order that, being thus weaned, we may learn to eat the bread, dry but more solid, of a vigorous devotion which is proved by being exercised in the midst of disrelish and temptations (*Introduction to the Devout Life*, pt. IV, chap. 15).

Rightly seen, the rigorous discipline which is undergone at such a time is an encouraging sign, for it shows that one is growing up and is no longer being treated as a child. One is being paid a compliment!

The director will often suggest suitable books for those who seek his advice to read, and he will dissuade from unwise or excessive reading of books of devotion. Praying is quite different from reading books on prayer—though the two are often confused. As much harm can be done by spiritual self-dosing as by physical self-medication through dipping into books on diseases and identifying one's own malady too impetuously. And just as doctors by no means always assume that their patients are suffering from the complaints the names of which they bandy about so confidently, so the priest will deal cautiously with penitents who tell him to which stage of the spiritual life they have attained.

But it is a great mistake to write off the spiritual writings of the saints as inapplicable to the needs of those who are struggling with elementary temptations or gross sins. The sinner and the beginner finds no incentive in mild spirituality or respectable behaviour. They need the saints, with all their exuberance and eccentricities, with all their burning devotion and absorption in God. St John of the Cross is not only an unparalleled guide in the spiritual life, but also a remarkable example of saintly living; and those who speak a trifle disdainfully of his mystical writings would do well to take a look at the events of his life. E. A. Peers gave an introduction to both in his book on the saint, *Spirit of Flame*, and some words in his last chapter will serve to underline the point being made.

Though a plain-dweller, I may travel to a land where I shall live many thousand feet above the level of the sea and find snow-capped peaks all around me. At first the change may not be easy to grow accustomed to, nor even pleasant; and, being no Alpinist, I may never in fact scale a single one of those peaks—only in a secondary sense will they become my familiar friends. But I shall soon become very different from the person I was in my home on the plain. From the keen air I shall draw greater physical wellbeing. I shall live more intensely; work harder, play harder and sleep harder. And it will be astonishing, even though I never become a mountaineer, if I do not soon find myself starting to walk up the nearest hillsides instead of being content with strolling along the valleys or the village street.

What is more, there will come a day when the valley is choked with drizzling mist and one side of the village street can hardly be seen from the other. What is it on that day that will inspire me to brave the rain and set out up the mountain path to see if I can climb above it into the sunshine? And, even if I fail, shall I not reflect that, if I lived in the plain, there would be no such opportunity? (p. 158).

On a more ordinary level it is necessary to insist that he who would give advice should know what he is talking about. It is far better to say nothing than to suggest a foolish or harmful course of action. There is the legendary bishop who advised the player of contract bridge that it would be all right if he played for sixpenny points—that is merely laughable. Not nearly so funny is the priest, vouched for by the late Father Gerald Vann, O.P., who advised a man who had committed homosexual acts to find a nice Irish girl and marry her; when the man received this advice without comment, the priest said, 'What's the matter? Don't you like the Irish?'[10] Similarly to pontificate about behaviour or speech in a factory without having worked in one and knowing nothing about the subject, is to invite amused contempt.

The priest should be on his guard against advice which starts, 'Don't'. This is not to say that warnings and prohibitions are unnecessary—far from it. But mostly people know that they shouldn't commit sins, and it merely adds to their discouragement if they are met with a blank prohibition. Nearly always reasons should be given for the prohibition, for a Christian should be trained to act intelligently and not merely to obey what somebody else says. It should be only exceptionally, very exceptionally, that one says, 'Don't argue: do as you are told: this is the teaching of Christ's Church.' The

[10] G. Vann, Moral Dilemmas, p. 67.

repetition of the question, 'Why?', can be irritating, no doubt; but the confessor's aim is to educate people to maturity of conscience and not to maintain them at the level of docile children. Something is amiss if people don't want to know why things are right and wrong, or if they are helpless without a lead being given. 'Why not judge for yourselves what is right?' (Luke 12.57). The author of 1 John is to be imitated. 'It is not because you do not know the truth that I am writing to you, but rather because you know it already.... you do not need anyone to teach you; the anointing he gave teaches everything' (1 John 2.21, 27).

If he is wise, the priest will notice how often he uses the second person as he gives advice. The bossy type will be always saying, 'You ought to do this: you must not do that.' It can convey the suggestion that the priest is immune to such temptations. The priest can make his point equally well if he puts himself on a level with his penitent and normally says, 'We ought always to be careful' or 'We should never behave like that'. On the other hand, the priest is wise if he does not obtrude himself, however much it may be the fruit of humility. The penitent does not wish to hear the priest's confession, and the confessor does well in general to avoid mentioning his own personal temptations, sins, failures, or successes. He may do so exceptionally, and then the very rarity of it may well make a deep impression on the penitent and bring the message home to him.

4

The administration of the sacrament

ITS PLACE IN THE PRIEST'S TEACHING

'What God wants is for you all to be holy' (1 Thess. 4.3): this is the theme to which the parish priest must continually recur as he teaches his people. No one can say that Jesus did not set the highest ideal before his followers: 'You must therefore be perfect just as your heavenly Father is perfect' (Matt. 5.48); and the parish priest must do the same. But he will not be convincing if he only talks about perfection; it will be in so far as he himself is striving towards perfection that his people will acquire the same eagerness. And it is only as he himself is trying and failing and trying again that he will be able to bear with the inadequacies of his people.

The priest must see that there is a difference between a man who is striving for holiness and a model parishioner. The incumbent is anxious to see his church well attended, to have keen people on the church council, and to have all the parish organizations well manned. But gratifying as this would be, it is not the same as the 'perfection' to which he should seek to lead his people. If he is sensitive to the needs of the individual, he will often have to deny himself the satisfaction of enlisting an active new parishioner in the interests of the man or woman in question. Just because someone makes his confession, he is not therefore to be bullied into coming to Evensong. Spiritual perfection is not the same as regularity at church and sacrament, even though the latter is or may be the road to the former.

Eagerly as he may desire to commend the practice of going to confession, the parish priest must see that it is only a means to an end, even if an important means. He must commend the practice as part of something greater—the total dedication of oneself to the service of God, a greater sensitivity to sin and deeper contrition, a firmer resolve to amend one's life. These are the important objectives, and the priest has not failed in his duty if many of his people are following along this road, even if, for one reason or another, none of them comes to him to confess his sins. Putting it the other way round, one has known priests who have imagined that their work was done when people became regular penitents (as also when they became regular communicants). But both priests and people need to remember that sacraments are means and not ends, and that it is notoriously easy to be content with the employment of the means without pressing on towards the end. Did not Pascal quote that terrible sentence (on which all parish priests should frequently ponder) 'Christians are people who with the aid of certain sacraments evade the duty of loving God'?

Against the background, then, of the preaching of sin and redemption and sanctification, the priest will commend the practice of sacramental confession. He will make no secret of it; he will announce publicly that at certain fixed times he will be in church to hear confessions (it is better to call a spade a spade and avoid paraphrases about 'spiritual counsel' and the like). Not only will he announce such times (which should be at least weekly), but also he will be unfailing in his attendance for that purpose. Many times, especially in country districts, there will be no one to avail himself of his ministrations, but at the least he will have some time for the refreshment of his own soul and for the meditation and spiritual reading that otherwise get crowded out of a busy life. And one never knows who will turn up, to whom one's priestly ministrations will be of untold value. Such fixed times will of course be added to before the big festivals. Both the usual times and the additional ones should be exhibited in the church porch and printed in the parish magazine. It should also be clearly stated that other times are available by appointment.

In the more traditional parishes it will still be valuable before Christmas and Easter to read the First Exhortation which follows the Prayer for the Church in the Prayer Book Communion service. Though not exactly modern in its style and approach, it expresses its meaning cogently, and those who hear it will at the least be forcibly reminded of sacramental confession and some may be led to inquire further on the subject. Some incumbents may prefer to say the same thing in their own words. This may have the more direct appeal, but there is the danger that the subject may be thought to be the 'high church' fad of the vicar rather than the express teaching of the Prayer Book. It is better to preach courses of sermons from time to time on the subject of sin and repentance rather than be always dragging in references to confessions in sermons on other subjects. No one likes being nagged, and it is a pity if it is thought that one has a bee in one's bonnet on the subject.

It sometimes happens that newcomers to the parish are unused to the current ceremonial and ask to have it explained. It is possible then to extend the instruction to other points on which they may be imperfectly instructed, confession and absolution among them. It also sometimes happens that a man will turn up saying that he is thinking of becoming a Roman Catholic. It may be that what he is seeking is absolution for his sins, and imagines that the only way to procure this is in the Roman Catholic Church.

Instruction about confession will be given to children, but the parish priest will probably think it sufficient to give instruction leading to actual confession only during their preparation for Confirmation. In many parishes it will be wise to make clear beforehand to their parents something of what is involved, e.g. that they will be expected to attend the Sunday Eucharist, that they will be taught about sin and confession, that it will be left entirely to them whether they make their confessions or not, that naturally they will also be given some elementary instruction about sex, and that they will be given the chance to join the free will offering. Such an explanation to the parents avoids difficulties later on. On the other hand, in parishes where the parents seem little concerned with the details of their children's instruction and are prepared to leave everything to the parish priest, it may be thought unnecessary to consult them specifically about confession.

There are those who emphasize the truth of the words of the wise man, 'Instruct a child in the way he should go, and when he grows old he will not leave it' (Prov. 22.6). If when young one has learned about confession and absolution, it may come in very useful many years later. But there is a danger in pushing children into making their confessions before they are fully alive in conscience; and it must be admitted that some adults are held back from the confession which they need because their early confessions were not understood or deeply felt. Much depends on the teaching and example of the parents.

It will be found useful to require candidates for Confirmation to examine themselves carefully about their sins, and a whole class can profitably be given to writing out confessions. The individual priest must decide whether to use a simple printed or duplicated list, or whether, instead or in addition, to explain things in his own way. Children's consciences are odd things; in some ways they may be very sensitive, in other ways totally insensitive, and much patience is needed. For example, they may find it hard not to believe that the totally accidental breaking of something valuable is extremely serious, while ignoring the culpability of vicious selfishness. Or they may estimate the sin of lying by standards very different from those of adults.

Where sexual purity is concerned, it has long been held important to say nothing which would suggest sins unnecessarily to the young. But inasmuch as the modern adolescent has his eyes opened to the so-called facts of life earlier rather than later, it is important that instruction about personal relations and sexuality should be given in plain language and in a matter-of-fact way. Many young people who appear sophisticated and knowing have a very partial and distorted view of the whole matter, and are greatly helped by a cool and realistic approach. But, as with other sins, there should be no bringing in of unnecessary detail. If there is an act of impurity, all that is requisite is that it should be mentioned, together with the statement that it was alone or with someone else, male or female, married or unmarried.

It is particularly necessary with children and young people to emphasize the need for contrition. It is not a straining of the feelings but an act of the will. It is not enough merely to list the wrongdoings. If it is sometimes necessary to speak bluntly, it is important to avoid anything approaching anger. One is rarely wrong in being optimistic and encouraging.

The priest should go cautiously with those who come to put up the banns, even when the bride is stated to be pregnant. For it is hard for a young couple who are deeply in love and have always intended to get married to feel that anything is very seriously wrong if sexual intercourse has taken place before marriage. Certainly he should not assume that here is an opportunity for pressing the desirability of confession on people who will be eager to listen. Mostly the reverse is true, and unless the couple are well instructed it will usually be best only to touch lightly on the matter. Otherwise the impression, already too widespread, may be given that the only sin the Church recognizes or is interested in is sexual irregularity. On the other hand, marriage is so obviously a new and important chapter in one's life that there may well be the desire to be forgiven the sins of promiscuity in the past so that by God's help all may be fair for the days that lie ahead.

What was said above about the need for patience with children applies also to the confession of the simpleminded and mentally disturbed. Both firmness and love are required, and it may be necessary in some cases to insist on sexual sins being dealt with very briefly and due attention being given to other sins.

In his teaching, the parish priest will always stress the importance of sincerity and completeness in the confession : unless it is going to be undertaken in the right spirit, it is better not undertaken at all. Yet he must be aware that incomplete confessions are often made; he should occasionally refer to this in his preaching. It is always desirable that this point should be made in a parish mission or at a special time such as Holy Week, when contemplation of our Lord's Passion will often convict someone of sin in this respect. It can be most appropriately and effectively done by a visiting missioner or preacher, and much good is done if he himself can hear confessions, since if there have been serious omissions it is easier for the penitent to go to someone other than his own confessor. A sacrilegious confession is a matter of such seriousness that it is far better for the penitent to take the easy way of going to a stranger than to be confronted with the more difficult task of going to the usual confessor and to be too cowardly to do so.

When a penitent confesses to having made an incomplete confession in the past, he should be treated not with severity but with especial kindness. It is hard to admit to past evasions and suppressions of the truth, especially when, as so often, what has been passed over is some sexual offence; and the priest should rejoice that the Holy Spirit has stirred the penitent to a true acknowledgement of guilt. Since it was fear that previously made the penitent insincere, it is vital to show that such fear was totally unwarranted, and that even the worst sins can be acknowledged at the foot of the cross without embarrassment. Tenderness at such a time speaks more eloquently of the wonder of God's love than almost anything else.

It may be wise to ask, 'You fully understood what you were doing when you concealed this, did you? Sometimes people persuade themselves that it is not wrong, or only realize afterwards how serious it is.' For though there is such a thing as deliberate concealment, there is also a state of uncertainty whether a thing is wrong or how wrong it is. It is particularly important to emphasize this when a penitent made his first confession ill-instructed and fumblingly, and only becomes aware years afterwards how inadequate it was. As with other questioning, the priest when faced with a disclosure of serious sin must not too readily assume that even so the full truth has been disclosed; and if there is any ambiguity, he should still ask whether it was something much worse that was done or not. Even in admitting to having concealed the truth, a penitent may not find it easy to admit the full extent of the concealment, and will go away with a conscience still unquiet if the opportunity for fuller disclosure is not given.

A general confession is sometimes to be recommended, quite apart from the question of the concealment of sins in the past. When a particularly decisive step is about to be taken, for example before ordination, before marriage, before taking religious vows, it is good not only to confess the recent sins since one's last confession, but also the sins of one's life. This can be productive of greater insight into one's condition and of deeper penitence and firmer purpose of amendment. It will not be prompted by any doubt about forgiveness in the past, but will be indicative of present humility and zeal. If, however, the penitent is known by the confessor to suffer from scruples, he will refuse to allow such a general confession to be made, since it is likely to be productive of harm to the penitent.

Many parish priests will want to encourage their people to make their confessions regularly : that there should be at least an annual 'spring clean' makes obvious sense. But in the first half of life once a year is very infrequent, and it is best to suggest a quarterly rule— before Christmas, before Easter, at midsummer, and at Michaelmas. This divides the year up reasonably well and is easy to remember. In some cases a priest may well suggest monthly confession, for it is easy to become discouraged in living the Christian life, and what to the individual seem insuperable obstacles and arguments for abandoning the Faith can be shown by the confessor to be familiar temptations which must not be met with despair but with courage and hopefulness.

It depends largely on the personality of the priest whether and to what extent he gives his younger penitents reminders about their confessions. From some priests they are received as the most natural thing in the world, but on other lips they seem accusatory or querulous. At all costs the priest must avoid nagging people. Perhaps when the visiting preacher in Holy Week says exactly what he has been in the habit of saying, people will take notice and respond; and the parish priest must be content to be the prophet unhonoured in his own country. He will not complain to others about his parishioners' slackness in this matter. If they seem remiss, he will pray for them with all the greater love and faithfulness. And patience is often rewarded.

II

THE PRIEST'S JURISDICTION

Every priest has the power to absolve. This is made abundantly plain in the formula of ordination:

> Receive the Holy Ghost for the office and work of a Priest in the Church of God, now committed unto thee by the imposition of our hands. Whose sins thou dost forgive, they are forgiven; and whose sins thou dost retain, they are retained. And be thou a faithful dispenser of the Word of God and of his holy Sacraments; In the Name of the Father and of the Son and of the Holy Ghost. Amen.

The sentence based on John 20.23 is not essential for priestly validity. It was only introduced into the Ordinal in the Middle Ages, and an ordination to the priesthood would be valid without it. (It is absent from the Roman Catholic Ordinal of 1968.)

Power is one thing, but authority to exercise the power is another. Hence the ordaining bishop proceeds:

> Take thou authority to preach the Word of God, and to minister the holy Sacraments in the Congregation, where thou shalt be lawfully appointed thereunto.

A priest is not at liberty to preach or minister the sacraments wherever he chooses, but only where the diocesan bishop gives him authority. By virtue of his institution to his benefice the vicar or rector has the needful authority; assistant priests minister according to the regulations of the bishop and the directions of the parish priest. It is customary for the bishop not to give priests permission to hear confessions until they have been three years in priest's orders.

During this time they commonly receive instruction to equip them for this task.

However, it is generally recognized that in case of emergency a priest, though he lacks authority or jurisdiction, may hear a confession 'in respect of any person who is in danger of death or if there is some urgent or weighty cause' (Canon B 29.4)—though the Canon deals only with jurisdiction. It is often useful if the bishop's permission can be obtained to enable a young priest to hear the confessions of children in his care, since he may well be in closer touch with them than his incumbent is, and they may more readily turn to him for help.

It is of academic interest only to inquire whether a deacon may absolve, or whether a layman may; for the mind of the Church is against allowing the practice. Perhaps they did so in the past, or did deacons only release people from ecclesiastical penalties? And if layfolk absolved, was this rather in the context of spiritual advice and brotherly correction? These are obscure questions and of little practical relevance. But it should be noted that the fact that priests undoubtedly have the authority to absolve, in no way proves of necessity that no one else has.

Whom may a priest absolve? Only those who are baptized. In the case of candidates for baptism, he should hear their confessions and instruct them that forgiveness of sins will be effected through the sacrament of baptism. He will give them advice and encouragement, but will not impose a penance or absolve.

He absolves in relation to sins committed after baptism. If the confession is so inadequate as not to reveal any sins, prudent questioning will probably reveal some and absolution can then be given. Otherwise the person should be given a blessing.

May he absolve only those who belong to the Church of England and churches in communion with it? Strictly he has no jurisdiction in respect of others. But inasmuch as members of other churches with whom the Church of England is in partial communion are admitted commonly to Holy Communion, it seems clear that they may also receive absolution. Thus a member of the Church of Sweden would rightly be absolved. But what of Methodists or Presbyterians in this country? It is unrealistic to label them schismatics, and to refuse them absolution until they are prepared to join the Church of England. On the other hand, they do belong to bodies separated from the Church of England, and one does not want to encourage them to be disloyal members of their denominations. In the present climate of opinion it would seem preferable to give absolution to such persons, and the fact that they ask for it implies some sort of recognition of the priest's jurisdiction. Pragmatically there can be little doubt that such exercise of discretion or economy tends to the healing of our unhappy divisions.

What of the confessions of Roman Catholics? They should be warned that their action in coming to an Anglican priest would be frowned upon by most of their own priests, and advised to confess to one of them. But if they insist and there is good reason to do so, the Anglican priest should give absolution.

In any of these cases where he has some scruple about the correctness of his action, the confessor may introduce the condition, 'if I have the jurisdiction to do so'.

III
HEARING OF CONFESSION

Confessions are normally heard in church. Unless there are good reasons for doing otherwise, this rule should be adhered to. Though only two persons are concerned, the priest and the penitent, the giving of absolution is an official act of the Church and should take place openly where sacramental rites are normally administered. People sometimes plead for a 'private baptism', but the reasons they urge for it are usually not convincing. Similarly though a confession can be heard anywhere—in the vestry, in a priest's study, out of doors, in hospital, or in the penitent's home, these are less suitable places than the church itself. For what is desired is the penitent's reconciliation with God, and there may be a danger of this being forgotten if without cause all takes place in less formal surroundings. These are all right if someone only wants to get something off his chest; they are all right if he wants to be assured that the vicar bears him no ill will; but it greatly helps the penitent to see that the important thing is his relationship with God if there is the degree of formality which is involved in going into the church building. The priest wears surplice and purple stole.

There are, however, many exceptions to this rule. The sick and the dying are in a class apart, and so are the deaf. On particular occasions the church may be too far away or its temperature too cold. Or the priest may judge it best to seize the opportunity presented to him rather than risk a delay. T. A. Lacey, who was no mean spiritual guide, once wrote that the absolution which he had given with completest assurance was to a cowman who confessed his sins to him, walking behind his cattle.

When a confession is heard in church, it is unnecessary and undesirable to wait until everyone else has gone or to turn people outside. The only people it may be desirable to remove at least to a distance are those who before a festival are engaged in decorating the church with flowers. If the organ is being tuned, it may be possible to get the tuners to voice the quieter stops for the time being. Where many confessions are heard, a grille separating priest from penitent may be useful; but mostly the priest will sit beside the penitent's prayer desk.

Before he sits down for the confession, the priest should kneel for a few moments and say some such prayer as the collect of Trinity 19. Then he takes his seat, and when the penitent has knelt, he pronounces a brief blessing, asking that a good confession may be made (see p. 1). If, however, the penitent has already started his confession, the priest will of course omit the blessing.

There is no set form for making one's confession, but it is desirable to have a printed card containing the words introducing and following the confession printed on pp. 1-2.

Though not strictly necessary, it is undeniably useful if the penitent says when his last confession was. If he fails to do so, the priest may reasonably intervene at once and ask whether he remembers when his last confession was. An approximate answer is quite sufficient—'two or three months ago', 'some time last year'. But if a penitent says, 'My last confession was a long time ago', it is useful to discover what this means, whether many weeks, many months, or many years. So the priest will ask (increasing the number for anyone elderly), 'Was it five or ten years ago?'—and usually it will be explained that it is a matter of months. If the penitent says he can't remember, it may be wise not to pursue the matter.

Patience and kindliness are called for, however long or however short the confession is. A very brief confession does not necessarily mean a superficial self-examination or a deliberate concealment of sins, and gentle questioning may elicit further material. At the other extreme it is disturbing when after half an hour of recital the middle-aged penitent goes on 'And when I reached the age of fourteen'; but it is probably best to let the penitent proceed in his own way, and only later on to make suggestions for conciseness in the future.

In the chapter on the preparation of the penitent, stress is laid on the value of encouraging the penitent to discover the defect of character from which his sins spring—whether he tells lies through vanity, laziness, cowardice, or malice. Some penitents confine themselves to recounting the plain facts without probing deeper, and it would be absurd in the confessional to try to discover the origins of all the sins confessed. But it can be advantageous when the penitent has finished, to pick out one of the sins and probe a little deeper. But the priest should phrase his question carefully. To say, 'What made you do that?', is unwise; it is a difficult question to answer on the spur of the moment, even if properly understood; and it is only too likely to produce the wrong type of answer, 'Well, my mother-in-law is terribly possessive and interfering'. Far better to ask, 'There are many different reasons why people behave like this. Do you think it was chiefly vanity that made you do that, or was it greed?' But there must be no harshness about the questioning; it must be conducted in a courteous and kindly spirit.

Some priests are in the habit of asking, 'Is that all?', at the end. No doubt it may elicit more at times, but to many ears it would sound either as though the priest thought there was more which was being withheld, or as though he were disappointed that so little had been confessed. If a priest has good reason to think there may be sins unconfessed, it is different; but here, if he has noticed that whole areas of sin have gone unmentioned, he may think it right to make a tactful inquiry. 'Many people in your circumstances find that they often yield to—this or that temptation. Have you sometimes given way to it, or is it a temptation which does not bother you?' Such a question will often greatly help a penitent who needed some sort of lead and will be glad of this assistance. On the other hand, a penitent will often disclaim anything of the sort on his conscience, and the confessor should at once accept his word and drop the subject. For if it is a sadness to a priest to have so much sin disclosed to him, it is also the greatest joy to have so much goodness and even saintliness unconsciously revealed—how much his own conscience is reproved by the amazing heroism and perseverance of some of his people! And it is in full accordance with traditional confessional practice that Bernard Häring writes: 'There are the numerous cases of "invincible ignorance" where pastoral gentleness and prudence realize that a "material" transgression of moral laws is a lesser evil—

no personal sin—than an outburst of rebellion or desperation that might be provoked by an inopportune admonition.'[1]

The confessor will often find it necessary or desirable to ask questions. While this may be resented by a penitent who is more anxious to conceal than to reveal his sins, in general it will be welcomed by the well intentioned. For they know that they are not very good at expressing themselves clearly; and for the regular penitent it can turn what may sometimes be a monotonous repetition of a habitual list of sins into something more living and meaningful. But the questions should be few, clear, and relevant. And it is better to err by omitting to ask many questions which should be asked than by asking one which should not be asked.

In most cases the priest will not interrupt the penitent to ask his questions, since he is then liable to get flurried and distressed. Especially is this so with penitents who speak rapidly. But with those who proceed more slowly, it is often better to interject a question at the time. Thus if a penitent says, 'I have failed to say my prayers' and then sighs and pauses for breath, it is easy to interrupt and ask, 'This was on many occasions?' The advantage of this is first that the priest does not then forget what he was going to ask; and, more important, it is a hint to the penitent to be more specific about frequency when speaking subsequently of his other sins. But more involved questions, seeking to determine motive, are better deferred until later.

Even in the matter of frequency, the priest will normally only ask questions about the more serious sins. But it may be diplomatic to make one's first question an easy one to answer, and to delay the more difficult one. 'When you said that you had neglected your prayers, you meant that you had left them out altogether? ... No, it was only sometimes? Ah yes. And when you said you had committed adultery, was this with several different people and many times? ... It was with one person and twice? Ah yes.'

The examples given have illustrated a point never to be forgotten. It is best to suggest by one's question that one assumes the sin to have been very grave indeed. It is easy then for the penitent to own up to something less serious. If the priest, out of a desire to help the penitent who confessed to adultery, said, 'It was just on one occasion?', the penitent would find it very hard to say, 'No, father, it was frequently.' Embarrassment and shame could easily lead to the

[1] *Norm and Context in Christian Ethics*, ed. P. Ramsey and G. Outka, p. 217.

penitent murmuring something noncommittal and then going on to the next sin. This technique should also be applied when a penitent professes to be unable to own up to a particularly terrible sin. If the priest asks whether it is something much worse than is probable, the penitent is usually able with relief to explain that it is not as bad as that, and that it is only—what it is.

It is often necessary to ask a question when the sin of stealing is confessed. 'I have often stolen things' is not specific enough. So the priest will say, 'When you said you had stolen things, was this big sums of money?'

It is often useful in connection with a first confession to ask, with reference to a particular grave sin, 'Did you know it was wrong at the time you did it?', and it can be explained that genuine ignorance can greatly reduce the gravity of a sin. In this way a disproportionate sense of guilt can be lifted from the conscience of one who has belatedly seen the wrongness of what was done.

IV

PENANCES

It is customary for a penance to be imposed and accepted before absolution is given. In earlier days the penance was a heavy penalty which had to be paid first, and then absolution was given and reconciliation effected. But for a long time now the absolution has come first and the penance, only a shadow of its former self, performed later.

It was reasonable that the Church should impose some sort of discipline upon an erring member in order to uphold its moral standards. Even if the discipline were only a temporary suspension of membership, it expressed the disapprobation of the Church for the sinner's misbehaviour, and it was medicinal for the sinner who was led as a result of it to a deeper sense of guilt and shame. Fasting and self-denial made contrition concrete; as John the Baptist had said, 'If you are repentant, produce the appropriate fruit' (Matt. 3.8). The more familiar version, 'Bring forth fruits meet for repentance', taken in conjunction with some passages from the Old Testament ('Redeem your sins by righteousness' (Dan. 4.27); 'Almsgiving saves from death and purges every kind of sin' (Tobit 12.9)), suggests a causal connection between forgiveness and man's deeds of 'satisfaction'. Though God's free forgiveness is still stressed, a theoretical basis for the necessity of works of satisfaction was found in the theory that there was still some temporal punishment due for sin—David was forgiven his adultery and murder, but the punishment for sin remained and his child had to die (2 Sam. 12.13-14)—and that this was remitted through the performing of penance. The result of all this was that, as Luther found, the teaching of God's free pardon tended to recede into the background, with the foreground occupied by human works of satisfaction and reliance on indulgences. The whole underlying theory was predominantly juridical and most unsatisfactory.

Why not then abolish even the modern attenuated penances? There is nothing unreasonable in this suggestion, for there is virtually nothing left of penalty in the saying of a collect. But there is something to be said in favour of retaining this small penitential exercise. First, it is a token of the new life on which the penitent is about to start; it outwardly expresses the inward resolve. Secondly, it is medicinal, being chosen for its appropriateness to the spiritual condition of the particular penitent. Far from substituting for the good works which are the fruit of Christian living, it serves to encourage and promote them.

Of what sort should they be? There must be nothing public about the penance given for secret sins; thus it would be wrong to tell someone to stop serving at the altar or singing in the choir for a month. Almost always it is best to impose a penance which can be performed before the penitent leaves the church—the saying of a collect, the reading of a psalm, the reading of a liturgical gospel, the repeating of a hymn. While it is reasonable to impose very light penances for small sins and somewhat heavier ones for grievous sins, it would be wrong to try to achieve an exact proportion. There should never be any suspicion of vindictiveness, and the less any idea of penalty emerges, the better. Even if the penitent asks for a heavy penance, it is unwise to agree. The heavier the penance, the greater the danger of thinking that the heaviness in some way 'atones' for the sin, when it does nothing of the kind. Far better to err on the side of light penances, even for grave sins; it is always possible to draw attention to the absurdly easy act of devotion that is required, in comparison with the grievous sins that are being forgotten. Christ's forgiveness is entirely free, and the penance is best seen as a grateful acceptance of forgiveness and token of amendment of life for the future.

The position is well expressed in the report, *Doctrine in the Church of England* (p. 198): The penance

> must be of such a character that it does not compel the penitent to make his offence public. Normally it is slight in character, and is not regarded as a penalty for the offence; it is prescribed and accepted in humble recognition and acceptance of the judgement of God, and as an admission by the penitent that his sin directly deserves punishment, even though by God's mercy that punishment is not exacted.

The priest should not give a vague penance such as 'make an act of self-denial' or 'meditate on the passion of Christ'; for a scrupulous penitent will be uncertain whether what he has done is a sufficient act of self-denial, and whether the meditation should be five, ten, twenty, or sixty minutes long. It should not be anything abstruse, like reading Tobit; if anything unfamiliar is required, the priest should make it plain where a Bible is to be found, and where the passage is to be found in the Bible. If a penitent has bad sight, it is unwise to ask for anything to be read; it is better to impose the penance of a prayer which can be said by heart. If a penitent demurs for some reason, it is better to substitute something which is more practicable.

Sometimes it is a good idea to recommend an act of devotion, while not imposing it as a penance. The penance itself should be something readily performable. 'As your penance, say the Lord's Prayer; but you might well, when you go to bed tonight, read Psalm 91 as part of your evening prayers. But this is only advice; don't feel badly about it if you don't.' Or, 'Say once as your penance the collect of the Sixth Sunday after Trinity; you may like to go on saying it every day next week. But that is not your penance; you will have done that when you have said it once.' By all means therefore recommend good devotional habits, but beware of imposing them as penances.

Through constant repetition of the Daily Office the priest acquires a good knowledge of the psalms and collects, and these will provide the bulk of the penances he gives. But hymns make valuable acts of devotion, and both children and adults find them profitable. The confessor should not however say only, 'Read hymn 206 as your penance'; it is best to specify the hymnal. Otherwise the priest may imagine that the *English Hymnal* is being used, when the penitent is using *Hymns Ancient and Modern*.

It is beneficial from time to time to give some help about the way to use the penance. 'As an act of gratitude to our Lord, read Psalm 34.' 'Read the Epistle for Quinquagesima, and think as you read it how splendidly it describes the character of Jesus.' 'Read Psalm 27, and try to carry the last verse away with you when you leave the church.' This should not be overdone, but it can be most helpful.

It is the custom of some priests before giving absolution to ask the penitent whether he has any question he would like to ask. Certainly it is a useful opportunity for clearing up doubts or difficulties, and it has something to recommend it. But it can be productive of anxiety or irritation for the penitent who never finds it necessary to ask questions, and perhaps it is better to ask the question only where there seems good reason to do so.

In the Middle Ages it was customary for absolution to be signified by the imposition of the hands of the priest, in accordance with one interpretation of 1 Tim. 5.22.[2] This custom has died out. But the priest customarily makes the sign of the cross in giving absolution. It is important, however, for the sake of the seal that this should not be visible. (For the same reason, should absolution not be given, it would be wise to give a blessing, making the sign of the cross.)

The form of sacramental absolution is prescribed in the Prayer Book in the Office for the Visitation of the Sick; discreetly modernized it will be found on p. 2. It has often met with objections. At the Savoy Conference the Puritans wanted it changed to 'I pronounce thee absolved, if thou dost truly repent and believe'; to which the bishops replied that the Prayer Book form was more agreeable to the Scriptures (John 20.23), and that the condition did not need to be expressed, since it was always necessarily understood.

As long as a similar form is used in Baptism ('I baptize thee'), and as long as the imperative is used in Confirmation ('Confirm,

[2] Thus the Homily on Common Prayer and Sacraments says: 'Although absolution hath the promise of forgiveness of sin; yet by the express word of the New Testament it hath not this promise annexed and tied to the visible sign, which is imposition of hands', and goes on to explain that it is therefore 'no such sacrament as Baptism and the Communion are' because this outward sign was not prescribed in the Gospels (The Second Book of Homilies, 'An Homily wherein is declared that Common Prayer and Sacraments ought to be ministered in a Tongue that is understanded of the Hearers' (Oxford 1859), p. 352).

O Lord, thy servant N.'—Second Series) and Ordination ('Receive the Holy Ghost for the office and work of a Priest in the Church of God'), it is reasonable for a similarly authoritative statement to be made in Absolution.

But it is foreign to the ethos of the Orthodox Church (cf. p. 14). Here at Baptism the priest says. 'The servant of God N. is baptized . . .', and absolution is given in the context of a prayer, 'Forgive now, O Lord, this thy servant N.'—except in the Russian Church, which borrowed 'I absolve thee' from the West in the seventeenth century. It would be mistaken therefore to regard 'I absolve thee' as essential. It is however psychologically preferable that absolution should be given with the greatest possible definiteness; and the wrong sort of sacerdotalism is surely excluded by the emphasis on our Lord as the fount of absolution and the Church as the depository of the power to absolve.

In case of urgent necessity the formula could be abbreviated to 'I absolve thee from all thy sins, in the name of the Father and of the Son and of the Holy Ghost. Amen.'

It will be a matter of opinion whether it is helpful to add to the Prayer Book formula such additional prayers as are to be found on pp. 2-3. While there is much to be said for a single clear pronouncement, there is also value in prefacing the absolving words with prayer to God from whom the absolution comes. In the earlier days of the Church these prayers were the form of absolution itself; 'I absolve thee' came later.

Absolution is followed in Roman Catholic practice by this prayer : 'The Passion of our Lord Jesus Christ, the merits of the Blessed Virgin Mary and all the saints, whatsoever good thou hast done or evil thou hast suffered, be to thee for the remission of sins, the increase of grace, and the reward of eternal life. Amen.' (It is however frequently omitted.) Without careful explanation it sounds as though Christ's Passion, the merits of the saints and men's own achievements were equally efficacious in contributing to forgiveness and salvation; and for this reason they are best avoided. They are, however, capable of a more orthodox interpretation. Men's good deeds are acceptable in Christ and may be called meritorious; and since we are members one of another, we must be able to benefit through one another's goodness. St Paul could say, 'It makes me happy to suffer for you, as I am suffering now, and in my own body to do what I can to make up all that still has to be undergone by Christ for the sake of his body, the Church' (Col. 1.24). But what is a deep spiritual intuition is distorted beyond recognition when suffering is imagined to be intrinsically efficacious, or when good deeds are thought of as items on a balance sheet, to be transferred hither and thither at somebody's good pleasure. The story of indulgence is not one of which the Church can be proud.

At a time when the corporate aspect of the forgiveness of sins is being recovered, one should not lose sight of our debt to the company of heaven. There is truth in both Thomas à Kempis's hymns; on the one hand he affirms:

> Every patient sufferer
> Who sorrow dared contemn,
> For each especial anguish
> Hath one especial gem.

Yet all is corporate in heaven:

> There the gifts of each and single
> All in common right possess;
> There each member hath his portion
> In the Body's blessedness;
> So that he, the least in merits,
> Shares the guerdon none the less.

Absolution looks backwards, so it is good to add a blessing which looks forwards into the future. For as a result of sacramental confession the penitent not only is released from the burden of the past but is given a flying start for the days that lie ahead.

And it is fitting that having discharged his ministerial duties in the name of his Master, the priest should acknowledge himself to be a sinner himself, and to ask the prayers of his penitent. 'Go in peace. The Lord has put away your sins. And pray for me, a sinner.'

V

MINISTRY TO THE SICK AND DYING

Sickness provides the parish priest with a great opportunity. When a man is removed from ordinary life and obliged to spend long hours on his own or with other sick people, he has the opportunity to reflect on the meaning of life and the use he has made of its opportunities. For the first time for many years, it may be, he has stopped to think, and he should be encouraged to believe that his sickness falls within the providence of God. Jesus deals with him as with the deaf man of Decapolis: 'He took him aside in private, away from the crowd' (Mark 7.33). If the priest is able to visit him regularly and they get on well together, he can suggest giving him some brief instruction on some part of the faith each time he comes—a refresher course for the somewhat nominal churchman, and one starting from scratch in the case of the complete outsider.

In the course of such instruction forgiveness of sins through Jesus Christ will be explained, and the way in which, through sacramental confession and absolution, this can be applied to the individual soul. Even if the instruction is given without immediate result, the time has not been wasted; prejudices have been removed and new insights given, and it may be years later that the seed sown bears fruit. The priest will be well satisfied if the patient acquires a deeper trust in the Saviour and a regular habit of prayer; though it is an important part of his ministry he must not get the promotion of the practice of confession out of proportion. Some will be indifferent, a few will be hostile, but there will be some to whom it will be a wonderful revelation of God's love.

It is when dealing with the dangerously ill and dying that the priest's work is most important and most difficult. If a man is likely to die, he needs to be helped so that with humble trust he can enter the presence of God. If his conscience is burdened, it must be relieved; if it is asleep, it must be awakened; if it is complacent, it must be directed to put its confidence in God rather than self. The principle of the directions in the Prayer Book Visitation of the Sick is that the priest should rouse the sick man's faith, stir his conscience, and bid him settle his affairs. He has the solemn obligation of 'moving' the sick man to make a special (i.e. detailed) confession of his sins 'if he feel his conscience troubled with any weighty matter' (i.e. mortal sin). It is not enough for the priest to be willing to hear a confession if asked to do so; it is for him to raise the subject and urge the desirability of confession if the sick man is uneasy in conscience. If the priest has previously tried to stir the man's conscience as the Prayer Book presupposes, it is very likely that something will be found to be weighing on his conscience for which he longs for the relief of absolution. (But it will be noted that absolution is not to be given to anyone who disbelieves in it or does not want it.) It must be clearly seen that the confession (and absolution) is not an end in itself; it is to be urged and used as indicative and expressive of the sick man's faith in God and his desire to love him.

One difficulty which the Anglican priest faces is the fact that most of the people to whom he ministers have little or no knowledge of sacramental confession. Things are a little better than they used to be, but in many quarters no heed is given to 1948 Lambeth Conference Resolution 110: 'Care should be taken to see that before Confirmation all candidates are given definite instruction about repentance and about the means provided by God in his Church by which troubled consciences can obtain the assurance of his mercy and forgiveness, as set forth in the Exhortation in the Order of Holy Communion.' Of course, if the sick person has made his confession before, it is easy for him to do so again; but the priest may usefully advise him that in his present state he need not feel it necessary to make as detailed a confession as he may have been in the habit of making in the past—let him confine himself to mentioning any big sins that stand out after a brief period of self-examination.

As with all ministrations to the sick it will be necessary to be alone with the sick person. Otherwise the priest's exhortations to faith and repentance are likely to be punctuated by a relative's assurances, 'Oh, he's a very good Christian', 'he's never done anybody any wrong'. Relatives too sometimes assure the sick man he has never looked better in his life when they know perfectly well he will be dead in a week.

Since nowadays it is customary never to mention the subject of death to anyone who is seriously ill, it is the more difficult for the priest to prepare the dying for death. But, particularly if he is preparing the sick man for the laying on of hands, unction, or Communion, he can stress the need to put everything in God's hands; if the patient is to receive healing for future service in the world, he needs to prepare as thoroughly as possible and to try to remove all that hinders God's purposes for him; and the same preparation is valuable if he is to leave this world for the nearer presence of God. It is his total wholeness that God wants—body, mind, and spirit—and the healing of one part of him reacts favourably on the other parts.

If, as is often the case, time is short, decisions have to be made quickly. The patient is probably unable to do more than respond briefly to the priest's questions about his sins—perhaps he may only be able to squeeze his hand by way of affirmative answer. If a penance is given (and it may often be dispensed with), it should be the simplest possible, such as repeating the holy name of Jesus. After giving absolution the priest may well help the penitent to joyous thanksgiving by repeating a well-known hymn such as *Jesu, lover of my soul*, *Abide with me*, *Rock of ages*, or Psalm 23.

5
The seal of confession

Never, directly or indirectly, may a priest reveal what he has learned
in confession from a penitent. Canon 113 (1603) required parish
priests to 'present' wrongdoers to their Ordinaries, but exempted
them from doing so if their knowledge of the wrongdoings came
through the confessional.

> Provided always, That if any man confess his secret and hidden
> sins to the Minister, for the unburdening of his conscience, and to
> receive spiritual consolation and ease of mind from him; we do
> not any way bind the said Minister by this our Constitution, but
> do straitly charge and admonish him, that he do not at any time
> reveal and make known to any person whatsoever any crime or
> offence so committed to his trust and secrecy, (except they be such
> crimes as by the laws of this realm his own life may be called into
> question for concealing the same,) under pain of irregularity.

The meaning of the exceptive clause is not clear. It has been
interpreted as requiring a confessor to disclose any type of treason:
but the Latin version of the Canon seems to imply that the reason
justifying disclosure is not danger to the priest but public danger—
civil war or the like. At the present time there is no crime the
concealment of which could result in capital punishment for the
confessor, and when a new Canon about the seal was being for-
mulated, there was no intention of including any exceptive clause.
   There is no reference to the seal of confession in the new Canon
B 29 of 1969—but this is not because the mind of the Church of
England is in any doubt. By an Act of the Convocations of Canterbury and York passed on 29 April 1959, it was agreed to be

> an essential principle of Church doctrine that if any person confess
> his secret and hidden sin to a priest for the unburdening of his
> conscience, and to receive spiritual consolation and absolution from
> him, such priest is strictly charged that he do not at any time

reveal or make known to any person whatsoever any sin so committed to his trust and secrecy.

As the Convocation debates showed, it was only legal complications which prevented this becoming part of the Canon. Though judges do not in practice require priests to break the seal of the confessional, it is a matter of legal dispute whether this is a matter of law or discretion.[1]

In ordinary circumstances if a priest is asked whether he knows some fact of which he has cognizance only through the confessional, he properly answers in the negative, since he is not being questioned about what he knows on that level. And if questioned about what he knew on that level, he would refuse to answer. The reason for this strictness is obvious. It would cut at the root of the whole ordinance if any discretion were allowed, and many who most needed to avail themselves of it would be afraid to do so if there were the slightest chance of anything in any way being revealed. They might well be afraid, not so much selfishly for themselves or their own reputation, as for others who would be affected by the revelation and their reputation. It should be noted that the death of the penitent in no way releases the confessor from the seal of confession. He must *never* use information so obtained.

The confessor cannot be too strict with himself. Doubt about people's reliability can be communicated not merely by saying things

[1] For a discussion of this question see Peter Winckworth, *The Seal of the Confessional and the Law of Evidence* (1952); *York Journal of Convocation*, January 1958, pp. 65-6, app. xxii-iii, and September 1958, pp. 45-51; and J. R. Lindsay, 'Privileged communications: communications and spiritual advisers', in *The Northern Ireland Legal Quarterly*, May 1959; also an article by Chancellor E. Garth Moore in the *Church Times*, 6 September 1963, occasioned by an *obiter dictum* of Lord Denning, Master of the Rolls, in the course of the Vassall Tribunal in 1963. 'Take the clergyman, the banker or the medical man. None of these is entitled to refuse to answer when directed by a judge.' Chancellor Garth Moore's conclusion was 'that the seal of the confessional of the Church of England is recognized by the law of England as inviolable, save, perhaps, in the one case, whatever it may be, excepted by Canon 113'. He reiterated his view in a letter to *The Times* commenting on an opinion expressed by the paper's legal correspondent (26 June 1973). A report of the Law Reform committee on privilege in civil cases (1967) recommended that priests should not be given the statutory right to refuse to answer a question that would violate the secrecy of the confessional. In giving evidence to the committee the Archbishop of Canterbury said it would be a help to the Church if privilege for confessions could be made statutory.

about them but by lifted eyebrows or by significant silence. It can be indirectly impugned by the dropping of 'discreet hints'—which in this connection would be entirely indiscreet and objectionable. The seal of the confessional would be broken if the confessor spoke of the sins *not* committed by a penitent, or if, hearing comparatively few confessions, he spoke in a generalizing way about sins frequently confessed. Though a priest may pray in private for a penitent's needs and may refresh his knowledge on particular subjects, he might unwittingly break the seal if after someone's confession he went to the local library to ask them to procure for him a book on alcoholism or lesbianism. He must not speak even to another priest about his penitent, even if he too hears the confession of the same person sometimes. Information about a third party given in a confession is also under the seal.

It is not always understood that the confessor must on no account speak to the man himself about his sins outside the confessional. He must not even in strictest privacy and with the best will in the world ask his penitent how he is getting on in relation to a particular sin or sins confessed. If the penitent himself raises the matter in conversation, that is different; it is clear that on this occasion he is releasing his confessor from the seal—but the latter must not assume that this applies to later interviews.

It would not be a breach of the seal, however, to add a few more words on a particular subject as the penitent rose to his feet after receiving absolution, since this would morally be within the confessional procedure. But this would not normally be done if there were other people waiting in church. Should the confessor speak to the penitent of his previous sins in a subsequent confession? This would not be a breach of the seal, but is a matter of the confessor's discretion. It may sometimes be helpful, but it is usually better not to do so, since the penitent may resent being questioned or nagged about a sin confessed in the past, and penitents would keep clear of confessors with unnaturally long memories. So instead of the priest saying, 'This is the third time you have done that!', it is preferable if he asks the question, 'Is this the first time?' or 'This is not the first time, is it?'

If a priest has knowledge of something outside the confessional as well as inside it, he is at liberty to use his knowledge acquired outside confession. But he should be particularly discreet in so doing, lest people should wrongly conclude that he was breaking the seal.

For it is important that unnecessary prejudice against confession should not be engendered.

The seal of confession binds anyone who overhears a confession, whether by accident or design, and anyone who finds a written list of sins left in church.

It is not part of the seal of confession that a person makes or has made a confession, since this is open to ordinary observation. But it would be breaking the seal to say that absolution had or had not been given or to reveal the penance. But a priest should not without good reason speak about the people whose confessions he has heard. This is a matter of ordinary good manners and discretion. It would be highly undesirable to say of someone who was about to appear in court, 'He made his confession to me last night'. It follows that a priest must not refuse communion to someone to whom he has denied absolution. He must not put a new lock on an alms box simply because a penitent has confessed theft and stated he possessed a key. He must not deter others from associating with someone whom he knows through confession to be a highly undesirable character. In all these cases he may and should put things strongly to the penitent and urge the proper course of action in the strongest terms; but more he may not do.

It must not be thought that all this imposes a great strain on the priest, to sort out professional knowledge from unprofessional. Mercifully, memories of what no longer concerns one fade into obscurity, and the priest who hears many confessions finds that they tend to vanish from the mind, almost without trace.

6

The preparation of the penitent

One of the confessor's chief difficulties is with people who seem to have little idea of what sacramental confession really is and who for a long time have made their confessions in an extremely defective way. He needs to be very patient with such people and tolerant of many shortcomings, since it is unreasonable to expect them readily to adopt a different attitude or employ a different method. But this makes it all the more important to ensure that those who approach confession for the first time should come after thorough preparation for it. Innumerable difficulties which would arise later on can be avoided if a proper explanation of what is involved can be given beforehand.

In the case of candidates for Confirmation this will mainly be done in the course of the ordinary classes, but it may be wise to refer to the matter again in the course of a personal interview with the candidate, since even today there is much misunderstanding and prejudice.

At other times when a priest suspects that one of his people is troubled in conscience and does not know how to resolve his difficulties, he should either invite him in for a talk and at some stage introduce the topic of sacramental confession, or (and this is often better) say : 'I should welcome the opportunity of explaining to you about confession and absolution. It's a thing many people know very little about, and I think you'd find it useful. But mind! Coming to have a talk about it in no way commits you—I certainly shan't expect you immediately to do something about it. It must be understood that you are under no obligation.' Even if the man says, 'Oh, I think I *want* to make my confession', the reply should be: 'No. You mustn't make up your mind until you know a bit more about it. When I've explained the thing fully to you, you may decide that if *that's* what it is, you don't want to have anything to do with it!'

In the first Appendix will be found a few points which frequently come up or which are especially important. Elementary truths should be repeated : that God is revealed to us by our Lord as a loving Father, infinitely forgiving; that Jesus himself *promised* never to turn away anyone who came to him (John 6.37); that in the words of absolution we hear the forgiveness of him who in his earthly ministry forgave the penitent sinner and who at the Last Day will welcome him into his eternal kingdom. Sacramental absolution reaches *back* to the earthly ministry of Jesus and *forward* to the Day of Judgement.

Most people are helped by preparing a written list or summary of their sins beforehand. How should they set about preparing it? A good self-examination list can be a great help, but an inferior one can be a great hindrance. The best ones help the person to see that sin is failure to show a virtue, and it is important to aim steadily at virtues rather than seek to avoid sins. Therefore those printed helps to self-examination are to be preferred which inquire the extent to which one has failed to display good qualities rather than those which concentrate the attention on the display of bad qualities. For sin is nothing in itself : it is failure to exhibit a virtue; and it is important to encourage this way of looking at things. For it is more important to see the attractiveness of virtue than the repulsiveness of vice.

It is often wise for the priest to recommend the penitent of mature years to divide his life into two or three sections. For he may have had a number of ups and downs; he may have started well, lapsed, and then returned to the faith. In such a case it would be helpful if it were clear whether the sin confessed belonged to a believing or an unbelieving period of his life; for it is one thing to miss one's prayers as a believer, but quite another as an unbeliever.

In connection with each sin the penitent should be told to give some sort of idea about frequency, and not just write, 'I have told lies'. Does this mean a few times at school, or many times every day? 'I have missed my prayers'—does this mean always, or once or twice? In order to be accurate, it might be expressed thus : 'I have very often missed altogether, and even since my Confirmation two years ago, it has been once or twice a week.' One should not encourage one's penitents to keep a sin ledger : 'I have missed 68 or 69 times' ! What is required is reasonable accuracy.

Penitents should also be encouraged to try to see *why* they sin in that particular way—*why*, not in the sense 'because my mother-in-law is so trying', but why in the sense of discovering the defect of character from which this particular sin springs. 'I've told lies, several times a week. Why? I suppose it's vanity; I don't like to seem inferior to other people, so I exaggerate and invent in order to seem equal to them.' Or it might be cowardice—to avoid getting in trouble. Or malice—in order to fix blame on someone who is an enemy. Or ambition—so as not to prejudice one's chances of advancement. It is here that printed lists of sins are often so unhelpful; they seem to be concerned only with the outward action and not at all with the vice from which it springs.

It is necessary to insist on this, even where the motive might seem to be obvious. Sexual intercourse with others may not be the result of yielding to sexual desire; it may be ambition that impels one, or revenge, or cowardice (not wishing to seem goody-goody), or many other things. It is essential if the penitent is to understand himself or get help from his confessor that he should not be content just to say what and how many times, but also (where possible) from what motive or motives. If the penitent does not know the motive, he is not to be pressed; but he should certainly be encouraged to look at it.

The penitent should be told to avoid all unnecessary detail. If he has stolen from a shop, it hardly matters which shop or on what day of the week. On the other hand, what he has stolen is important—and this should be stated clearly. A confession must be complete, or it is useless. It is grievously sinful wilfully to conceal sins in one's confession.

With intelligent penitents it is often a good idea to suggest that they prepare their confession as completely as possible, using their own intelligence, and then, when they think it is complete, to run their eyes over a list of self-examination questions. It is surprisingly easy for whole areas of sin to be absent from one's mind. (They may need a warning that not all 'sins' in such lists necessarily are sins; e.g. 'I have bought things on Sunday'.)

It is of the greatest importance to draw attention to sins of omission; they clearly figured largely in the mind of our Lord. But they are usually very difficult to remember. Being so selfish, human beings don't even see the opportunities they should have grasped.

Penitents sometimes need to be warned that it is not only sins which are worrying them that they should confess—though there is

no reason why these should not take precedence of the others. Their
aim must be to confess all their sins. But this is not completeness for
its own sake; completeness is required as a sign of contrition. Indeed,
whereas completeness without contrition would be useless, contrition
without completeness (assuming this to be accidental) is still precious.

Not infrequently someone preparing for confession will say he has
discovered sins which he is not sorry about. Often what he means is
that he cannot be altogether sorry about it. Often it is a sexual
liaison which he is reluctant to confess as a sin. What is often meant
is that there was so much good about something that it is hard to
confess it as a sin. An analogy often helps at this point. Suppose a
man broke into a house and stole some books; suppose that as a result
of reading one of the stolen books he was converted to the Christian
faith—would he later be sorry for having stolen the books? The
answer is that he would be sorry, since stealing is sinful; but he would
be glad that though the action was bad, God had allowed something
to happen as a result of it which was entirely good. In some such
way as this it is possible to show that one can genuinely repent of a
liaison which nonetheless added a new dimension to one's life. God
allowed good to come out of evil.

Penitents should be encouraged to mention sins which they
committed not knowing them to be sins. Sometimes no guilt attaches
to them. But the conscience behaves oddly. Instance the behaviour
of children on someone else's land who say, 'We won't go over there
and read the notice, because probably it says "Trespassers will be
prosecuted"; as it is, we don't know we are trespassing.' Many alleged
sins of ignorance are of this sort!

They should be told not to mention other people by name in
their confessions, for they are confessing their own sins and not other
people's. Obviously one cannot avoid allusions to one's parents,
children, teachers, employers, etc.; the point is that no unnecessary
specification of other people should be made. (It is true that anyhow
the seal of confession is absolute; but were this not made plain the
penitent might out of malice, conscious or unconscious, draw attention
to other people's sins in an undesirable way.)

In spite of all the present-day freedom of speech, some people
find it embarrassing to own up to sexual sins. The priest should be
matter-of-fact in dealing with this subject; often he will find it wise
to assure the penitent that it is very difficult to think of *original*
sins—they have all been recounted so many times before! There is no

need for irrelevant detail; but it is relevant to know whether a sin
was committed alone or with another, whether male or female,
married or unmarried; for someone to say, 'I have not always been
pure', would be totally inadequate.

An adult may remark jokingly that if he made his confession, it
would take a very long time indeed. Of course it is no light task to
discover the sins and failures of a lifetime. But the priest will anticipate this objection, if he is wise. He will point out that the man is
not setting out to write his autobiography; that in any case he is
bound inadvertently to have forgotten most of his sins; and that all
the irrelevant detail which makes an autobiography fascinating is
omitted in a confession. There one provides the bare facts with only
necessary additional amplification.

Forgetting is not usually deliberate—how can one deliberately
forget? But, as Jeremiah knew, 'The heart is more devious than any
other thing, perverse too: who can pierce its secrets?' (Jer. 17.9).
Nietzsche put it succinctly. ' "I have done that", says my memory.
"I cannot have done that", says my pride, and remains inexorable.
Finally my memory yields.' Unconscious self-love makes one forget.
This is why psychoanalysis is so painful: one is obliged to face what
one preferred to forget. It is clear that some (though not all)
outrageous liars have deceived themselves before deceiving others;
they cannot *believe* what they have done.

The penitent may be told that it is sad to be obliged to spend
time looking into oneself which might be spent looking at God. He
must not get fascinated with his own state of soul. St Teresa with her
usual common sense wrote: 'It is a great grace from God to practise
self-examination, but "too much is as bad as too little", as they say;
believe me, by God's help we shall advance more by contemplating
his divinity than by keeping our eyes fixed on ourselves.'

If the Christian life is like a walk in lovely mountain scenery,
then it is a pity not to spend all one's time enjoying the air, the
sunshine, and the views. But it may be an unfortunate necessity
to stop by the road, take off one's shoes and deal with the blisters
or other injuries which are diminishing one's capacity to enjoy.
While it is desirable to be thorough, one does not want to spend
more time on it than is absolutely necessary. If anyone seems likely
to be over-conscientious, the priest will be wise to tell the penitent
not to spend longer than an hour at the most, just as with those
suffering from scruples (see pp. 86-90) he should strictly forbid them

to spend more than fifteen or twenty minutes on an examination of conscience.

It has been necessary to speak at length of completeness of confession and the need to ensure that sins are not concealed. But there is something even more important, and that is contrition or sorrow for sin. If the penitent has the right attitude towards sin, he can hardly help confessing his sins with sufficient accuracy; the converse does not hold good. It is possible to confess sins with painful accuracy of detail and not be truly contrite at all. It is not only children who can own up to doing wrong without being sorry for it: adults too, including some of those who seek for absolution most frequently, can be sadly deficient in this respect. For one can, without thinking, fall into the belief that the recounting of one's sins is the all-important part of the procedure. Contrition and amendment have a very small place in the thinking of such people. So it is important to point out the need for contrition, and to explain carefully what it is.

Some people regret the consequences of their actions, wasted money, ruined health, imprisonment, social ostracism, broken marriage—whatever it may be. They wish they had avoided these dismal results of their actions. But this is not contrition—they merely wish that their actions had not had these consequences. It is a step forward when they accept these consequences without bitterness as inevitable, but it is still a long way from this to genuine sorrow at having offended God.

Others again feel remorse and cannot forgive themselves for having fallen the way they did. They are full of self-reproach and self-disgust. It is important that they should see that pride is at the bottom of this; whereas the Pharisee in our Lord's story betrayed pride in thanking God that he wasn't like other people, the sinner in this case betrays pride in saying how shattered he is to find that he is like other people—the image of himself as a nice person has been totally destroyed.

Others again, as will be shown in ch. 7, feel very guilty but are not really contrite. Like the character in Kafka's novel *The Trial*, they find themselves frustrated and unable to extricate themselves from an opaque situation: they are not aware of having made a mistake, or not a serious mistake, and yet since they are unable to make progress, they feel as if they must have made a grave error—

or someone in authority thinks they have made a grave error. Such guilt feelings have little to do with penitence.

> Sorrow [wrote Alban Goodier] is repenting for something wrongly done; it is a longing to put right the evil and injury; it is determining that the like shall never happen again; *and it is all from the motive of love.* Sorrow springs from love, or it is not sorrow ... Sorrow that is born of love has in it the immortality of love and can never die; on the contrary, the more with time the soul's eyes are opened and it sees what its sins have done, so much the more will it grow in intensity and in its effects.

When the saint seems to the sinner to be almost pathologically grieved by what seems a tiny sin, it is helpful to remember the analogy of the accomplished musician, whose slightly flawed performance grieves him, since he knows what the piece should have sounded like; the tiro has noticed nothing amiss, since for him it is wrong notes which constitute musical errors! So the saint has the spiritual finesse which is impatient of even minor imperfections.

Though it might be thought that by this time the penitent will be daunted by the magnitude of the task ahead, in practice this is not normally the case. For the procedure is seen to be eminently practical and sensible; there will obviously be no morbid poring over sin for its own sake; there is something appealing about the thoroughness involved; the confessor is in the best sense of the word a professional and is not going to fumble about in an embarrassed way. Best of all, the penitent is going to make plain to God that he means business, that he is taking Jesus at his word, and that he is coming confidently to the throne of grace. It is a paradoxical situation: on the one hand, 'It is a dreadful thing to fall into the hands of the living God' (Heb. 10.31); on the other, what could be better than to accept the invitation of the Good Shepherd, 'Come to me, all you who labour and are overburdened, and I will give you rest' (Matt. 11.28). There must be fear in the sinner's heart as he approaches the all-holy God; but he comes in order that he may hear the incarnate Son say, 'Courage, my child, your sins are forgiven' (Matt. 9.2). He is taking Jesus at his word, and coming to the minister of Jesus to receive the pardon of Jesus.

Mostly it is wise to make an appointment when a man's first confession is to be heard. If the church is one where many confessions are heard, a first confession is liable to cause unexpected and awkward delay for other penitents; still more, if the novice has to wait for twenty minutes while others make their confessions ahead of him, this inflicts unnecessary disquietude on him as he waits in some anxiety for what lies ahead. It is far better for a special appointment to be made. If even then he fails to turn up, the priest will without acrimony make another appointment. He knows that confession thought of beforehand can hardly seem other than an ordeal to some people; it is only afterwards that the 'ordeal' has been found to be an encounter with the merciful and loving Saviour.

It is extremely important that the priest who has been giving help to the penitent should not assume that therefore it must be to him that he must make his confession. (This will only be the case where he is the only priest for miles around.) It greatly helps the penitent to be told that he is free to go to whom he chooses. Most frequently he will inform the priest that of course he intends to make his confession to him; but from time to time he will have the salutory experience of hearing the person say, 'Oh, thank you. I dreaded the idea of coming to you; I shall go to Father B.' What does it matter, A or B, so long as sins are forgiven and someone is set on the right path?

Some people believe that it is morbid to go back into the past in order to renew the memory of sins long over and done with. It needs to be pointed out therefore that absolution transforms the past. It does not abolish the past, it is true; it does not even abolish the memory of the past. But it turns heaviness into joy. Even if the memory of old sins begins by producing melancholy and dismay, that it is not the last word. For though grievous sins induce gloom as the mind dwells on them, it is totally different with grievous sins *which have been forgiven.* The pain and sorrow associated with sin are neutralized and transformed by the joy that comes with the certainty of forgiveness. If my sins have been great, far from being permanently depressed and miserable, I shall go on my way rejoicing at the marvellous goodness of God who has forgiven me— I have more reason than most to be thankful and happy! Instead of being weakened in any good resolution as a result of past failures, the penitent is encouraged by the memory of God's gracious mercy in forgiving them.

Therefore sadness is no sign of penitence, rather the reverse, for it suggests a certain self-absorption. The penitent must give Jesus the credit of meaning what he says. If his sins are forgiven, then he must act accordingly. The prodigal son enjoyed the banquet prepared for him and his mind dwelt on his father's generosity; that was his way of showing appreciation. It would not have been a good sign if every five minutes he had interrupted the meal by telling his father again how bad he had been and how unworthy he was to be there. And yet, paradoxically, the prodigal, who in a sense was contrite when in his misery he made up his mind to return to his father, will have reached much greater contrition during the joyous festivities at his father's table. For the crucial thing is not our awareness of our sin so much as the experience of the Father's love.

It is sometimes necessary and often desirable for the penitent to do something to put right the wrong he has done. If he has stolen something, it must be restored—this can often be done anonymously. If it is a case of paying back a large sum of money, the penitent must at least make a start with an instalment. If there has been a quarrel, the attempt must be made to achieve a reconciliation by means of an apology or something of the kind. The confessor's advice is particularly useful here, since some apologies provoke trouble rather than make for peace. If there has been unfaithfulness in a marriage, should the offence be confessed to the partner in the marriage? This is by no means always the course to be recommended, even if the penitent wants to own up, for it may imperil a marriage rather than strengthen it; and the penitent may be advised to bear the pain of being thought to be more trustworthy than in fact he is, rather than to ease his conscience by putting an unnecessary burden on his wife's shoulders. Nonetheless, though he may be advised not to precipitate possible trouble by openly confessing, he must also be told that concealing the truth is one thing, but lying another—he is not entitled to deny what he has done.

If it is a case of the penitent forgiving someone else, he may need to be told that if it takes two to make a quarrel, it also takes two to achieve reconciliation. He may *want* to achieve a settlement, but the other may be unwilling. Or he may not be sure how much he *wants* to—can he be sure that he is in love and charity if rancour keeps rising in his heart? He must be told that though he cannot prevent such hostile thoughts coming to him, he need not welcome them into his mind: unwanted callers cannot be prevented from ringing your doorbell, but it is your fault if you ask them inside! So long as a man can pray for his enemy, he loves him; for he is saying to God as he prays: 'You love me and you love this other person; please go on doing so: that is just what I want.' And if, as is likely, the hard feelings return from time to time, the same remedy must swiftly be applied.

The resolve to do better for the future is a token of contrition. But the conscientious penitent is often unhappy about this—how can he be sure that he will not sin again? Is it not even probable that he will sin again? If so, how can he be said to be sorry? Such difficulties spring from an honest heart. The penitent must be told that he must purpose amendment of life, not promise it; the purpose of amendment, serious as it is, is not to be construed as a promise, still less as a vow. If later he succumbs again, that proves only that he is weak, not that he is a hypocrite. Where a sin is a matter of habit, it is often useful to aim at reducing the frequency of it. If the penitent seems to despair of conquering it, he can be encouraged to be thankful that his victories over the temptation are more frequent.

To some what has been said may seem too easygoing: but what is the alternative? The alternative is to dissuade anyone who is conscious of weakness from seeking absolution, lest a subsequent fall should convict him of hypocrisy. In other words, the people who most need the strength which the divine forgiveness affords are to be denied it! Only the most strongminded and only the people most ignorant of themselves would confess their sins if such foolish rigorism were to be adopted. And the person who relapsed into sin would feel unwelcome and might abandon his faith. It is usually pride and not honesty that makes a man abandon his faith in the face of moral failure—he would rather not try than try and sometimes fail. G. K. Chesterton's epigram is worth pondering: if a thing's worth doing at all, it's worth doing badly. None of us would be Christians at all if we had to make a great success of it. And if Jesus told his followers to forgive seventy times seven, is he going to ration his own forgiveness?

It is abominable to promise to try to do better if you have no intention of trying; and God is not mocked. But the priest must be very slow indeed to decide that a penitent is being dishonest. If he is inclined to do so, let him consider what the reason is for his censorious attitude of mind towards his penitent.

7
Special problems

SEXUAL SINS

There are some difficult cases which are quite likely to turn up and about which the confessor needs to know his own mind. For example, a man makes his confession, in the course of which it emerges that he has divorced his wife (or been divorced by her) and has married again. How is the priest to view this situation? Exceedingly little guidance has been given on this topic, and what follows is little more than a sketching out of different possibilities.

The confessor who adheres to the traditional teaching of the Church about marriage and divorce will regard the man as living in a state of mortal sin : with his first wife still alive he is habitually having intercourse with someone else. He must be admonished to bring his present union to an end and cease committing adultery. If there are children by the second union and it seems utterly wrong to end the second union, he must forgo sexual intercourse with his partner and they must live like brother and sister. For our Lord's teaching seems crystal-clear: 'The man who divorces his wife and marries another is guilty of adultery against her' (Mark 10.11). He may indeed be absolved in relation to these sexual offences which he has committed; but he cannot be absolved as long as there is this continuing situation of the second union. He is like the man who has stolen a large sum of money; he may be absolved from his sin, but not if he announces that he has no intention of returning it or even of trying to return it; the fact that he has no intention of turning over a new leaf indicates that he is not contrite. (See also pp. 22-26.)

The confessor who holds a different view of marriage would in such a case give very different advice. The first marriage is dead, and the second is alive; therefore the second union is not to be ended or weakened or deprived of its physical side just to satisfy a theological theory. (It should be noted that this confessor must be prepared to tell a wife who has been through the divorce court that her marriage is dead, and that she must *not* think in terms of remaining faithful to those marriage vows whereby she pledged herself to be true to her husband 'till death us do part', or of being prepared to forgive him and receive him back if he had a change of heart.)

The confessor who holds the second view may decline to be as logical as he should be; while not condemning the husband who has formed a second union, he may still wish to encourage the deserted wife to keep the door open for a future reconciliation, however remote such a possibility may seem to be. And the confessor who holds the first view of marriage may still see that other considerations enter in which will alter his assessment of the situation. Two in particular may be mentioned. First of all, there is the conscience of the penitent. If the penitent is (mistakenly or not) morally sure that he has done the right thing in forming a second union, does this make no difference? In any case some weight has to be given to the consideration of invincible ignorance, and further, since (however mistakenly) there are numerous voices in the Church, including those of some bishops, encouraging or at least condoning such second unions, is not the penitent entitled on principles of moral theory to follow such teaching, and is the confessor justified in insisting that unless the penitent accepts *his* teaching on the matter, he cannot be absolved? (And for a long time the Orthodox Churches have recognized divorce and remarriage as a second-best.)

Secondly, the fact has to be weighed that the Convocations have enacted that it shall be within the discretion of the diocesan bishop to determine whether to admit those who have contracted a second union after divorce to the sacraments. He is to do so if he is 'satisfied that the parties concerned are in good faith and that their receiving of the sacraments would be for the good of their souls and ought not to be a cause of offence to the Church'—and this decision is to be accepted as authoritative both in his diocese and in the whole province. If a diocesan bishop is able thus to declare that someone may receive baptism, confirmation, and Holy Communion, it is plain that such a person can hardly be denied absolution. Yet the priest is in the dark about the grounds on which absolution should be granted. Is it that the first marriage is dead? Or is it that in the circumstances the man is allowed to have a second wife? Or is it that if a man breaks the law 'in good faith', the Church must never deny him absolution? These unresolved questions place a heavy burden of responsibility on the parish priest. It would seem that since the Convocations have solemnly recognized the bishop's responsibility to admit to the sacraments of baptism, confirmation, and Holy Communion, it should rest with the bishop also to give absolution in these cases. The same grounds which enable him to admit to Holy Communion presumably enable him to absolve. This would mean the introduction into the discipline of the Church of England the system of 'reserved cases'; no priest would be competent to absolve in such cases, and the parties would be advised to go to the bishop for absolution (see p. 25).

A similar area of doubt may be thought to arise in the absolution of practising homosexuals. Often they accuse themselves of sexual sins with members of their own sex and promise to try to steer clear of these sins for the future. But there are those who are living together in a relationship not of lust but of love, and who declare that they do not and cannot regard it as wrong to express their mutual love in bodily intercourse. What is the confessor to say? Those who regard 'good faith' as the crucial test would presumably give absolution, together with any priests who dissented from the traditional teaching of the Church in this matter. But the majority of confessors would be unwilling in general to push the plea of good faith so far, and would decline to agree that 'there is nothing good or bad but thinking makes it so'. If the individual himself is the sole judge, what is the purpose or rationale of sacramental confession? What are the limits of conscientious refusal to accept the Church's teaching? Here, it should be noted, there is no such substantial body of informed opinion to justify departure from the traditional teaching, nor have any who would urge such a departure given an adequate rationale to justify it. Further, often but not always those who claim to have a clear conscience about their behaviour in this matter will be found to have an unacknowledged uneasiness; and the confessor can reinforce this judgement, while showing himself gentle and understanding towards those whose make-up makes these 'unnatural' activities 'natural'. They are right in seeking companionship and love, for few people are called to be hermits; there is a great measure of fulfilment along these lines, and if these are achieved, half the battle is won. For promiscuous sexual behaviour is often a sign of inability to form stable personal relationships at any level.[1]

[1] For further discussion of this difficult problem see H. Kimbell-Jones,

It would generally be agreed that conscientious divergence from the Church's teaching should be respected by the confessor on matters of secondary importance—on what is deduced from first principles. If there is divergence on first principles, the penitent cannot expect a minister of the Church to condone such a serious difference. In such a case he must be warned that it is a matter of weight, and that he must seek to be guided by the Spirit of God, and that so long as he is truly doing so, God will not hold him guilty of wilful sin. But he must honestly study the question, and not ignore the fact that the weight of Christian teaching and experience is against him. The trouble, however, is to decide which are the matters of first principle and which are the less certain deductions. He who is rigorist by conviction will tend to expand the former category, and he who is more liberal will tend to expand the latter category. Only the study of competent books on moral theology will enable the confessor to proceed as he should in his ministry on behalf of Christ and his Church.

II

THE SCRUPULOUS PENITENT

In the lives of the saints one reads not only of their love for God but of their sorrow for sin. Having glimpsed the holiness of God, they are convinced that they are the worst of sinners. This is not affectation, for they are more clear-sighted than the ordinary run of men and are less deceived by self-love; they have realized something of the extent of God's loving concern for them, and are appalled at the tiny extent to which they have responded to it. Given their advantages, they should have made such vast progress, and this they have failed to do. Therefore they regard themselves as chief of sinners.

The inexperienced priest may wrongly think that he has come across such a person when he finds a penitent with a super-sensitive conscience. (Often he is a man, but more frequently it is a woman who shows these characteristics.) She is in despair at her lack of love for God, and instances it in a variety of ways—she has deliberately allowed her mind to wander to other things when at prayer; she

---

Towards a Christian Understanding of the Homosexual; Sherwin Bailey, Homosexuality and the Western Christian Tradition (Longmans 1955); and N. Pittenger, Time for Consent (SCM 1967).

has failed adequately to realize the presence of God; so often she has said her ordinary prayers over three or four times because her praying has been so culpably unconcentrated. She cannot be sure that her motive is pure love; there is so much selfishness in her approach and so much thought about what others will think. Her very confession is all wrong; she has spent so little time preparing for it, only two or three hours, and she has been so lacking in real desire to know the truth about herself and so easily satisfied with what is merely superficial.

After half an hour or more of listening to this sort of self-accusation the priest may think that here is someone on the road to sanctity; but in fact the penitent is suffering from scruples. 'Scrupulous' can be used in a good or a bad sense. The apothecary used the word 'scruple' to denote a twenty-fourth of an ounce; if a medicine would be useless in too small quantities and lethal in too large quantities, one would be glad before taking it to know that it had been 'scrupulously' dispensed! But if one was buying a hundredweight of potatoes, it would be annoying to be delayed for a long time while the vendor scrupulously secured that he was supplying exactly a hundredweight, with not even a fraction of an ounce too much or too little. This would be to be fussy.

The scrupulous penitent fusses about matters of minor importance, and thus betrays a faulty conception of God, who is thought to be equally concerned with these matters of minor importance, and a vast self-concern, for it soon becomes clear that what she is trying to satisfy is less the will of God and more her own perfectionism. To aim at perfection is excellent, but to be despairing as long as something is not perfect is folly. The man who is hygienic is careful to wash his hands; but the man who is a pathological case washes his hands a hundred times a day in case he has touched something infected.

The ignorant outsider tends to regard the scrupulous penitent as a case of 'religious mania'; but in fact those who are not religious can also be affected in this way. The psychiatrist is accustomed to dealing with them. The confessor, far from encouraging this super-sensitivity of conscience, will see such a conscience as a sick one and will try to restore it to health. The practice of sacramental confession should help to remedy such scrupulosity, not to encourage it.

The scrupulous penitent is sick, and therefore the priest should be compassionate and not censorious. He needs great reserves of patience, for the scrupulous can often be extremely provoking and difficult, and it is hard not to blame them for their demanding ways. But, as they sometimes realize, they are suffering from their scrupulosity, and sufferers should receive sympathy rather than blame. Yet it must be a wise and strong sympathy which the priest shows and not a weak one, for no one is more expert than the scrupulous penitent at exploiting her confessor's weakness. Firmness is essential.

In the ordinary way the confessor is always seeking to train the penitent's conscience, and the penitent is helped to follow the Holy Spirit's guidance as this is perceived by his spiritual faculties. The confessor is always seeking to reduce the importance of his own role. But the trouble with the scrupulous penitent is that her conscience itself is sick and not to be relied upon; and the only path to a sensible and fruitful life is by trusting the wisdom and experience of the confessor implicitly. So long as the penitent's own conscience is so unreliable, she must trust the direction of one whose conscience is recognized as reliable.

Thus the priest will insist that, for example, prayers shall be said once only, and that on no account shall the penitent repeat them in order to say them better. He will insist that the time spent on them shall be fifteen minutes, no more and no less. He will lay down a length of time which is not to be exceeded for the examination of conscience. The penitent finds it very hard to give this necessary obedience. Like the inveterate alcoholic, she can always find an excuse for making an exception: in general the rule is right, but on this occasion and in these circumstances ... ! And when challenged the penitent will want to go into lengthy explanations to show that she is right and the priest is wrong, or rather, that the priest is wrong because she has not properly explained all the ramifications. Patiently the priest must explain that he does understand and has taken it all into consideration, and still he insists on his rule being adhered to. He may have to be blunt. 'If you insist on doing something different, you must stop consulting me or making your confession to me.' And if the penitent is afraid that she is committing sin by being thus obedient, then the priest must tell her to offer her obedience to God, and to put all the blame (if blame there be) on the priest—God will understand.

But the penitent is not by any means sure that God will understand ! She is self-absorbed and is unwilling to give up her own ideas, and her own spiritual progress and perfection are of supreme importance—in the last resort even God has to take second place. It must be understood that this is a factual description of the typical scrupulous penitent, not a judgement on or condemnation of her. For it is a malady and not perverse priggishness which produces it, and whatever rational arguments may be adduced to show that the scruples are vain, there is an emotional attachment to them which is hard to displace.

It requires a full acceptance of God's love and forgiveness for this abnormal state to be cured. For the penitent is bent on establishing her own righteousness and thereby earning the love of God. She must see that the inexorable tyrant is her own super-ego, not God whom she seeks to placate. There is some truth about herself which she is unwilling to face, and rather than face it she submits to this slavery to scruples which is demanding enough to divert all attention from other duties. If she can be led to face what she is afraid of, and come to terms, it may be, with forces and feelings whose existence she will not admit, then a new life can start. If she can forgive herself, then she will be able to accept the wonderful truth of God's forgiveness.

It will generally be found that the scrupulous person is not sorry for her sins, even though she expatiates on them at some length—she feels guilty about them, and this is very different. She is conscious of having failed to live up to her own ideals, still more of having failed to live up to ideals which have been inculcated in her by some-one else. Accordingly, even to be assured in the most solemn way of God's forgiveness may bring little relief, since the penitent is grieving about failure to achieve a standard, not failure to love God. If God forgives her, then that is weakness on his part, for she herself has a higher standard of behaviour than God! It is therefore essential that sin should be seen in the framework of personal relationships, and analogies from human life should be frequently adduced. It might be pointed out, for example, that a mother would much prefer to have an affectionate son who was often selfish rather than a frigidly upright son who showed no love for her at all. And only the experience of love can evoke love. As Harry Williams wrote: 'When a man feels that somebody accepts him, blemishes and all, without any sort of strings attached, then for that man the Kingdom of God has drawn near with its power to heal and raise from the dead.'[2]

[2] *Traditional Virtues Reassessed*, ed. A. R. Vidler (SPCK 1964), p. 12.

The scrupulous person has little sense of humour—that is part of the trouble; and the priest must take care not to seem to laugh at her troubles. If he tries to lessen the tension by making a humorous comparison, he must take care to include himself in the joke. 'I expect you are like me, you would hate to pick up a frog in your hand. We know that it is perfectly harmless, yet we can't bring ourselves to do so. Fortunately it doesn't much matter, and we humour ourselves by not picking frogs up, even though we know it's silly to have a horror of frogs. So don't worry about these anxieties of yours: accept them as one of your little superstitions and stop trying to fight them. Think instead about giving pleasure to your next-door neighbour, or do some knitting for your nephew.'

A priest's patience will often be severely tried, but he must not lose his good humour or become fierce. If the scrupulous person comes regularly for encouragement, it may often be wise at the outset to state the limit of the interview. 'I am glad to see you, but at three o'clock you will have to go, as I have some important things to do.' And be firm as well as gentle when three o'clock comes. If no limit is prescribed, the priest may get more and more enraged as the time goes on, and any attempt to stem the flow of words will be misinterpreted as a form of rejection. Sometimes a penitent knows she is being unreasonable, and because she is a burden to herself, realizes that she must also be a burden to others; and it is tremendously helpful and reassuring to be always met with love and understanding. This applies not only to the scrupulous, of course, but to all who are self-distrustful, for one reason or another. As Izaak Walton remarked in his *Life of George Herbert*, 'It is some relief for a poor body to be but heard with patience'.[4]

III

PATHOLOGICAL CASES

The chaplain in the mental hospital has to deal with people every day who are abnormal or pathological cases; and there are books to help him in his ministry.[3] Here consideration is not being given to the regular care of such persons in hospital, still less to their therapy or the alleviation of their disabilities. But the ordinary parish priest

[3] Notably Norman Autton: *The Pastoral Care of the Mentally Ill* (SPCK, 2nd edn 1969).
[4] World's Classics edn, p. 292.

may expect to come across some extremely disturbed people in the course of his ministry, and he needs to have some ideas about the manner in which he should minister to them.

There are two policies which he should avoid. He should neither assume total responsibility for such people, combining the roles of priest, medical practitioner, and psychiatrist, on the one hand; nor on the other should he wash his hands of them completely and make a quick escape from embarrassment. He must minister to them, as to everyone else, to the best of his ability; he will be wise to recognize how limited his ministrations are bound to be in such circumstances. But just because they are limited, he must not assume that they are non-existent.

First of all, he must show elementary courtesy. His instinct, it may be, is to run away, because he is disconcerted by the person who comes to him and he feels unable not only to solve their problems but even to cope with the situation at all. But at least the priest can be patient and courteous. The man in question is likely to have met with a great deal of unkind or brusque treatment from others, to whom his condition presents a security threat; so it is something at least if from a minister of Jesus Christ he receives unafraid and gentle consideration. For he is not just a case, still less a monster or an animal; he is a person, albeit suffering from depersonalizing maladies.

Secondly, it is Christ's own courtesy he must show. There will probably be little or no opportunity to speak avowedly in the name of Christ, but it will be in the name of Christ that his minister can welcome one who is dear to his Master, whatever he may be according to human estimates. Here more than anywhere else, it is what a priest is that counts, rather than what he says. To use modern jargon, he constitutes an official Christian 'presence' for the distressed and distraught, and he should restrain any eagerness to improve the occasion with a message. A silent prayer or a spoken blessing may well be preferable.

Thirdly, he will absolve such a person, whatever defects there may be in the confession of sin or the admission of guilt. For example, such a person may well confess to having started a world war. A priest can hardly absolve someone from the guilt of a totally imaginary sin; but he may perhaps be able to elicit one or two other sins which truly have been committed, and then, stressing the total character of the divine forgiveness, he can give absolution. It is usually a mistake to argue or try to prove that a sin is imaginary, still less to pooh-pooh it and refuse to take it seriously. Absolution is not likely to remove the load of guilt from the conscience of the deluded person; but it counts for something at least that the terrible truth (as it appears to be) has been told and God's priest has refused to be disconcerted by it, but has pronounced the words of absolution.

The same policy should be adopted if the penitent is obsessed by sexual sins, true or imaginary. There should be no discussion of the content of the confession, but only a loving and un-nagging direction of attention to the Saviour's love. The priest may judge that his penitent is the victim of compulsive action, but should accept the fact of such infinitesimal guilt there is and absolve. It is no comfort to a sick soul to be told that his actions were without guilt because they were unwilled by him and therefore blameless !

The word *penance* is best avoided, because of its misleading associations. If the penitent should demand a penance, it is preferable to avoid the subject and instead say : 'After your absolution, there is only one thing I want you to do, and that is to say, just once, *Glory be to the Father and to the Son and to the Holy Ghost*. Will you do this?' and as soon as the penitent says yes, immediately to cut further discussion by giving the absolution and blessing. With the necessary qualifications a similar line should be taken with those who are mongol, retarded, or otherwise mentally incapacitated. Everything should be put in the simplest possible way. Hymn-verses are useful, and short phrases from the Gospels, frequently repeated.

8

A re-examination of sacramental confession

I

THE CORPORATE ASPECT OF CONFESSION

One of the criticisms often made of the present administration of sacramental confession is its markedly individualistic character—it is a case of 'my sins being forgiven me'. Now there is nothing untrue about this way of looking at things, but it is markedly one-sided. Baptism confers a spiritual rebirth, but it is a rebirth into a new family; in the Eucharist the individual receives his communion, but it is communion and fellowship not just with Jesus but with the Body of Christ. It needs therefore to be stressed that sin itself is not only an offence against God but against one's fellows, reconciliation must be sought not only with God but also with one's fellows.

This can be achieved in a number of ways. It is possible to stress the fact that the confessor is not only the representative of God, bearing Christ's commission, but also the representative of the Church, one who is also a sinner, and also one who by the penitent's sin has been sinned against. By his sins the penitent has failed to maintain the witness which a member of the Christian Church should give; whether in secret or in public he has helped to reduce the spiritual temperature of the community of which he is a part. So he has failed his brothers and sisters as well as his heavenly Father. A small step in this direction would be made if the recommended formula introducing the confession were not just 'I confess to God' or even 'I confess to God and before the whole company of heaven', but 'I confess to God and to the whole Church of Jesus Christ' or something of the sort. And the confessor, if he judges it to be appropriate, can stress the corporate aspect of sin and forgiveness when he gives advice.

In a closely knit community it is possible to go further and for acknowledgement of failure in love to be made either to the community as a whole or to the individual members chiefly concerned. (It is not suggested that *all* sins should be thus confessed, but only those which have plainly affected mutual relations.) The Chapter of Faults in a religious community is different, since it concerns only breaches of religious discipline, but it points the way to what could be done on occasion.

In this connection Dietrich Bonhoeffer comes to mind, both because he himself felt led to confess his sins to one of his own ordinands, and also because on one occasion he particularly impressed upon his students the desirability of confession one to another as a preparation for communion.

> Soon after, on a Saturday evening, Bonhoeffer talked to us about confessing, brother to brother. There was to be a Communion service the next day. In deep earnest he spoke to us, stressing the urgency of it, but leaving us the freedom of personal decision. He said if we wished to be free, we would have to make a clean breast of the grudges we bore one another ... So on this evening we went to see one another, and spoke of the many grievances stored up in the last few weeks. It was a great surprise to realize how we had hurt the other person, without intention, by chance, almost *en passant*. Now we knew what it meant to consider other people. The atmosphere was pure again, we could go to communion together without bearing a grudge against anyone among us. We were never given such a 'starting-signal' again, but the beginning which was made continued in many pastoral conversations. (*I knew Dietrich Bonhoeffer*, ed. W-D. Zimmerman and R. G. Smith, p. 109).

Some Roman Catholic priests are also experimenting with corporate services of penitence. Here there is no specifying of individuals' sins, but a corporate acknowledgement of failure which, while less specific than an individual's confession would be, goes deeper and is more challenging than the sort of 'general confession' customary within liturgy. Though this helps to meet a particular Roman Catholic need which is not felt in the same way in the Church of England, yet it is possible to apply and adapt it to Anglican use. For it enables the conductor of the service to focus attention on the sins of society, whether the society be Church or State or class; and though it is not easy meaningfully to repent of sins about which one can barely promise amendment of life, it is certain that such sins weigh heavily on the consciences of many people to whom the small individual sins of daily life seem relatively insignificant. It also helps to release people from the too common idea of atomized sins emerging from an otherwise exemplary life, and to expose their sin-ridden condition.

In former days some parish priests attempted some such service of penitence when, perhaps in Holy Week, they sought to deepen the penitence of the faithful in preparation for their Easter communion; it might serve too to bring some to make a sacramental confession. It may well be that there is a place for some such exercise today. Or, taking the hint from the old Commination service appointed for Ash Wednesday, one might make the beginning of Lent a time for challenge to self-discipline, less on old-fashioned individualistic lines (giving up sugar in my tea) and more on a corporate application of Christian justice and love towards some sections of the community in which the congregation lives and witnesses.

In some cases the service of penitence is followed by a mass hearing of confessions in the ordinary way by a number of priests; in others the service ends with an absolution being given in response to the carefully prepared general confession. Theologians are divided on the subject of the quality of this absolution—is it sacramental or not? Before this question can be answered, it is necessary to consider the status of the precatory absolution given in the course of liturgical services and (for Anglicans) the declaratory absolution which precedes the Daily Offices. Perhaps the Doctrinal Commission may be asked for an answer to this. As regards the Roman Catholic Church, the Dutch Catechism, modern as it is thought to be, denies the sacramental nature of such absolution after only a general confession,[1] but it is affirmed by some Roman Catholics in Canada, among other places.

Another way in which Christians can be helped to a better use of confession is by enabling them to see that the particularized sins which they mention are only symptoms of a deeper malaise. We have done what we ought not to have done—that is fairly readily observed: we have left undone what we ought to have done—that takes a lot of discovering; but the real trouble is that there is no health in us. There is something wrong with everything that we do—not in the sense that everything that we do is totally wrong, but

[1] A New Catechism, 1967, p. 460.

rather that there is at least a smear of self-love about all our actions. A perfect action can only proceed from a perfect person, and we are far from perfect.

Whereas reciting a familiar list of sins can be rather soul-destroying, if it is supposed that I am right except for these trivial sins, it can still be of value if they are seen to be an inevitably superficial particularizing of what can be detected on the surface of the soul— the very fact that these weeds come up shows that there are deep and widely-ranging roots below the surface.

It is therefore worth quoting the experience of the Russian pilgrim described in the second half of the anonymous *The Way of a Pilgrim*. Though because of its generalities it is not a model for the confession of the individual, it assists the penitent to see that he is called to holiness and not just to respectability, and allows him to see his sins as instances of a more profound worldliness and godlessness. The pilgrim in the book had shown the ascetic priest the paper he had written, containing the sins he wanted to confess. The priest dismissed it as useless, and gave him some notes to bring him to a proper state of humility. 'For', he said, 'you have not acknowledged nor written down that you do not love God, that you hate your neighbour, and that you are filled with pride and ambition.' This is a summary of the notes in question.

I *do not love God*. For if I loved God, I should be continually thinking about him with heartfelt joy. If I loved God, then talking with him in prayer would be my nourishment and delight, and would draw me to unbroken communion with him. But on the contrary I not only find no delight in prayer, but even find it an effort. If one person loves another, he thinks of him throughout the day without ceasing, he pictures him to himself, he cares for him, and in all circumstances his beloved is never out of his thoughts. But I throughout the day scarcely set aside even a single hour in which to sink deep down in meditation upon God, to inflame my heart with love of him, while I eagerly give up twenty-three hours as fervent offerings to the idols of my passions.

I *do not love my neighbour either*. If I did love him as myself, misfortunes would distress me also, his happiness would delight me too. But on the contrary, I listen to curious, unhappy stories about my neighbour, and I am not distressed; I remain quite undisturbed, or, what is still worse, I find a sort of pleasure in them. Bad conduct on the part of my brother I do not cover up with love, but proclaim abroad with censure.

I have no religious belief, neither in immortality nor in the Gospel. If I were firmly persuaded and believed without doubt that beyond the grave lies eternal life and recompense for the deeds of this life, I should be continually thinking of this. I should lead this life as a foreigner who gets ready to enter his native land. Were the Holy Gospel taken into my heart in faith as the Word of God, I should be continually occupied with it, I should find gladness in the study of the Law of God day and night. On the contrary, if now and again I read or hear the Word of God, I usually come to the end of the reading without any profit, only too ready to change over to secular reading in which I take more pleasure.

I am full of pride and sensual self-love. All my actions confirm this. Seeing something good in myself, I want to bring it into view or to pride myself upon it before other people or inwardly to admire myself for it. If I notice a fault in myself, I try to excuse it, I cover it up by saying, 'I am made like that' or 'I am not to blame'. I get angry with those who do not treat me with respect. In a word, I continually make an idol of myself and render it uninter-rupted service, seeking in all things the pleasures of the senses, and nourishment for my sensual passions and lusts. (From *The Pilgrim Continues His Way*, 1973 edn, pp. 24-8.)

And another pilgrim can point the way forward more positively. Walter Hilton in *The Scale of Perfection* gives a lengthy description of the Christian life as a pilgrimage; it is summarized by Augustine Baker in *Holy Wisdom* (I. vi). Here is an extract.

There was a man that had a great desire to go to Jerusalem; and because he knew not the right way, he addressed himself to one that he hoped was not unskilful in it.... The other answered that the way thither was both long and full of very great difficulties ... Nevertheless one way he knew which, if he would diligently pursue according to the directions and marks which he would give him—though, said he, I cannot promise thee a security from many frights, beatings and other ill-usage and temptations of all kinds; but if thou canst have courage and patience enough to suffer them without quarrelling or resisting or troubling thyself, and so pass on, having this only in thy mind and sometimes on thy tongue, *I have nought, I am nought, I desire nought but to be at Jerusalem* ... thou wilt escape with thy life and in a competent time arrive thither.... Thy principal aim and indeed only business is to knit thy thoughts to the desire of Jesus, to strengthen this desire daily by prayer and other spiritual workings, to the end it may never go out of thy heart.

II

CONFESSION AND PSYCHIATRY

It has sometimes been glibly asserted that if more people had availed themselves of the opportunities offered by the confessional, the consulting rooms of psychiatrists would be empty. Certainly it is true that many people's lives are poisoned because they have never been shown how to face the truth about themselves or to believe in the possibility of forgiveness and a new start, and no one should undervalue the great power of pardon freely given and freely received. But all the same there is more falsity than truth about that assertion. There is plenty of work for psychiatrists even in places where people regularly confess their sins and receive absolution. The priest needs to be clear about the difference of his approach to the sinner from that of the psychiatrist.

The unsophisticated view of human beings is something like this. Man has some impulses towards good, and other towards evil; or he is like the charioteer with a pair of horses, one pulling one way, one another; or he is possessed of free will and must decide whether to listen to the good angel whispering in his right ear or to the bad angel whispering in his left ear. On this view of man the priest's task is to help remedy the wrong choices made and to encourage the making of better decisions for the future; he is to point to the ugliness and destructiveness of sin, and to the beauty and creativeness of virtue. Socrates believed that goodness flowed from knowledge: we needs must love and follow the highest once we really see it. Hence men's paramount need for healthy and rigorous education.

But it is surprising how much evil remains after years or centuries of teaching. And as the psychiatrist sees it, the priest only too often is like the medical practitioner urging his patient to take plenty of food and plenty of exercise, when in fact the patient has stomach ulcers which make eating painful and a broken leg which makes walking impossible. Only after the man's inside has been put right and his leg put in a splint and set, is he able to profit by the excellent advice previously given to him. No doubt it was of *some* service to have told the dyspeptic man to eat heartily—so long as it was only certain specified foods; it was of some service to advise exercise—so long as it did not involve standing on the broken leg; but neither piece of advice was particularly helpful so long as the basic trouble had not been dealt with.

Similarly, the priest may admonish the alcoholic to be strong-minded; he may tell the kleptomaniac truly enough about the loveliness of honesty; he may bid the homosexual cultivate relationships with the other sex—all in vain. For the psychiatrist sees the priest's client as needing cure rather than exhortation. For it is not wilful perversity that makes the first man drink alcohol to excess, or the second man to steal, or the third man find physical satisfaction with members of his own sex; these people are virtually unable to do anything about their condition, or if they can, it is very very little. They need treatment rather than blame, and a cure more than pardon.

Plainly priest and psychiatrist need never compete with each other if the former deals only with perfectly balanced people and the latter only with pathological cases. It is because most people fall between these two extremes that they are liable to misunderstand and mistrust one another. When the psychiatrist seems to the priest to be treating his client as *only* the victim of circumstance, the priest complains bitterly that the client is being robbed of all sense of responsibility and told not to think sinful actions which are plainly wrong. On the other side, the psychiatrist is liable to complain that the priest is only making his work difficult or impossible by fostering guilt feelings in his client and refusing him the autonomy which would enable him to stand on his own feet. Yet it is disastrous if either interferes with the other.

Is the solution then to increase the number of priest-psychiatrists or psychiatrically trained priests? Much good undoubtedly comes when men have a real competence in both branches of study; of all men they know the great value of both disciplines. But it may be doubted whether these hybrids point to the solution. For though a priest can also be a psychiatrist, he cannot function simultaneously as priest and psychiatrist—he must play one role or the other. In classical psychoanalysis the psychiatrist is a non-directive listener; he wants his patient to talk and to talk freely; he abstains from moral judgements; even in his questions he tries not to suggest the answers. To describe him, however, as dispassionate would not be correct, for he has a concern for his client.

It is hard to see how a priest *as priest* can play this part. For he is known to be a man of God; he represents the supreme authority; he upholds the teaching of Jesus Christ and of his Church; whether he welcomes or repudiates the title, he can hardly help being in some sense Father to the person who comes to him. However much in abeyance it may be, therefore, a directive role is implicit in his calling. He may, he will, eschew the role of the 'heavy father'; he will not refuse discussion and demand blind obedience; but in the end it is as an agent of the God who can claim man's total surrender and loyalty that he will appear.

Perhaps the contrast has been made too sharply, since the priest is also a fellow Christian, a fellow human being, a fellow sinner, and it is much to be desired that he should in no way hide or soft-pedal this. If he is Father, he is also brother; indeed, he who is Father knows what it is to be a son who has left home and turned prodigal, and to need and receive the divine forgiveness. 'He can sympathize with those who are ignorant or uncertain because he too lives in the limitations of weakness' (Heb. 5.2). But the priest who is true to his calling dare not be content to meet people on the human level—or rather, he may *meet* them on the human level, but it will be in order to enable them to raise their eyes to a higher level. The sympathy and patience and forgiveness and hopefulness that he exhibits will not be just those of another human being, but will be those of the Only Son of the Father. No one thought less of self than Jesus, and he moved with ease among the outcast and distressed; but through that emptying of self the presence of the Father was the more manifest. 'Go away!' said Peter to Jesus on one occasion; yet paradoxically it was from Jesus that Peter on another occasion refused to go away (Luke 5.8 : John 6.67-8).

The difference can be put in another way : the priest is concerned primarily with the conscious mind, the psychiatrist primarily with the subconscious or unconscious. The priest is the musician eager to assist the pupil; the psychiatrist is the piano-tuner who makes it possible for the pupil to play—or he is the doctor who cures the deafness or paralysis which impedes the playing. The psychiatrist as a psychiatrist is no more concerned with what his client makes of his life than the piano-tuner is concerned with the sort of music played on the instrument which he has tuned. Since the psychiatrist is a human being as well as a professional man, he will have his own ideas about human living; but he will be a bad psychiatrist if he allows his beliefs to emerge.[2]

People often ask to be recommended to a Christian psychiatrist—and presumably they would regard a priest-psychiatrist as best of all. But if the position has been correctly set out, the thing for a patient to look for is a good psychiatrist, i.e. a qualified and competent one. In principle a Christian psychiatrist is no more and no less desirable than a Christian dentist—yet few people go round looking for Christian dentists. Two things lie behind the request. One is the implication that the client doesn't at any price wish for his existing way of looking at things to be disturbed—but perhaps it very much needs to be disturbed; perhaps an infantile religion needs to be reduced to rubble in order that the ground may be cleared on which in due course an adult religion may be erected. The other thing however is that the client may rightly be unwilling to entrust himself to a psychiatrist who would have no scruple about imposing his atheistic ideas on his client, under guise of being thoroughly scientific. But what is needed (as always) is to avoid the quack, the crank, and the shark, and to entrust oneself to someone really competent.

III

CONFESSION AND COUNSELLING

What relation has pastoral counselling to the traditional sacramental confession and absolution? In one sense, a great deal, since by means of each Christ's love for the distressed is made concrete. It might be thought that whereas the practice of sacramental confession used to be, and to some extent still is, a matter of serious dispute between Christians of different allegiances, the practice of 'counselling' involves no theological disputes and can be agreed on by all as a valuable service which the pastor may be expected to supply. No such lengthy period of rigorous training as the psychiatrist receives is demanded of the would-be counsellor; the counsellor is not expected to probe the unconscious, for his concern is with the same area of human existence as the confessor's. Surely then they can learn from

[2] There is a clear differentiation of the roles of priest and psychiatrist in R. S. Lee, *Freud and Christianity*, p. 37.

each other—perhaps even the counsellor can be expected to supersede the confessor.

Certainly the more that practitioners of different kinds come to understand one another's approaches and techniques, the less they will be separated by walls of prejudice. It is highly desirable that confessor, counsellor, and psychoanalyst should trust one another, and, if possible, meet in order to compare notes. But just as the view was put forward above that it is virtually impossible simultaneously to play the parts of psychiatrist and priest, so it would seem that there is a similar incompatibility between the roles of counsellor and confessor.

For in the modern jargon, 'counselling' means, not giving counsel! It is of its essence to be non-directive, and the priest can hardly help being in some ways directive. This view is put forward strongly by R. S. Lee in his *Principles of Pastoral Counselling* in the SPCK Library of Pastoral Care; and it is not unfair to Lee to summarize his position as favouring the role of counselling rather than that of confessor—though he looks forward to a time when confessors will view their task more in terms of counselling. Another writer in the series, Kenneth Preston, in *Marriage Counselling*, takes a pragmatic view, with which Lee would hardly agree, urging the parish priest to use his discretion whether to be directive or non-directive. In other words, he urges him not to be so set on his role of 'non-directive counsellor' as to fail to see the duty of 'directing' in certain emergencies. Perhaps Lee is more logical than Preston : he advises any priest who recognizes that he is the paternalistic type of character to keep clear of counselling; he can be a good pastor in his own way, even though he may not be equipped in his own personality to be a good counsellor. Preston envisages the priest of a parish having to give advice on marriage problems, and he advises him to go a long way in following the counselling method, while still preserving a flexibility of role.

One source of confusion needs to be pointed out. It is clear what 'non-directive' means—but what is the opposite? 'Directive', it may be said. Yes : but there is direction and direction, and the confessor may be anything between the extremes of heavy authoritarianism and of near-non-directionism. Even Lee, carefully as he writes, does not always remember this. For example, he writes (p. 116):

In confession it is the spiritually and psychologically mature penitent who is most able to gain from it. The disintegrated and mal-developed are more likely to become fixed in their weakness, yet it is these who, judged by their actions, are the greater sinners. They stand in greater need of counselling. It would be going too far to say that saints need confession and sinners counselling, but there is enough truth in it to give point to the saying.

The point is worth making, certainly, and there is much truth in it. But there is an underlying suggestion that the confessor purveys only one medicine and that a directive one to all his penitents, mature or immature, integrated or disintegrated. But in fact the confessor has a variety of medicines at his disposal, and is not likely to treat the immature as mature; in practice he may well achieve much the same result as he reduces to a minimum the amount of direction he gives, as the counsellor would achieve with his non-directionism. In the less severe cases it is possible through the confessional to help lead the immature on to maturity, and a priest will often rejoice when a hitherto dependent penitent decides to dissent from a line of conduct suggested by the priest.

This is not by any means an argument against counselling or in favour of shepherding all to the confessional. Many people need the counselling approach and should be discouraged from making a sacramental confession. Still more is it true that many should be discouraged from the counselling approach and entrusted to the psychiatrist. Stress is only being given to the fact that the priest's 'directive' approach would be better if less elegantly described as 'non-directive'. The opposite of total abstinence from alcoholic liquor is to be a drinker, no doubt: but 'drinker' can hardly help suggesting that the person is a heavy drinker! Similarly being *directive* is too liable to imply being heavily directive.

Is it necessary to defend counselling? Since many of people's troubles spring from an unconscious unwillingness to admit the truth about themselves, the only way to enable them to get to this truth is by a *total* absence of condemnation or blame. Only when a man accepts the whole truth about himself can judgement begin, and the judgement will be self-administered, with the priest at his side concerned to take his attention away from the calculus of wrongdoing and to direct it instead to the total acceptance of the wrongdoer by the ever-gracious and welcoming Saviour. Perhaps an analogy will help. In an ordinary family both praise and blame are given, and children, far from being injured by this, are helped to mature. But a deprived child who has become delinquent may well require an environment of total acceptance and of total absence of blame or punishment, if he is to come to terms with himself and be able to enter into personal relationships. Only when integration in some measure has been achieved is it possible to talk in terms of praise or blame.

In other words, a sick person needs a cure, rather than blame for being sick. If the priest has a tendency to blame too much, the psychiatrist often goes to the other extreme of denying that anyone should be blamed. According to Lee (p. 114) repentance

> is an honest facing of the facts, the recognition that not only have we done something bad, but also that we could not have done anything else at the time; that the sin expressed our true nature and we are helpless to do the good we see.

Hence 'the sin must be accepted and loved with the sinner' (p. 93). Is this so? It is unnecessary to decide 'whether men are sinful or sick' (p. 94), for they are usually both. In one's treatment of the well-integrated person, one regards his actions as predominantly voluntary and responsible (while remaining aware of the compulsions to which all are to some extent liable); in one's treatment of the disintegrated person, one regards his actions as predominantly compulsive and any adverse judgement is suspended. Just because blame would be ruinous for the latter type, it does not follow that it is inapplicable to the former; and just because the former is rightly regarded as responsible, it does not follow that the latter must be so regarded. If it is wrong to go round dispensing blame indiscriminately, it is equally wrong to go round indiscriminately acquitting of blame.

It is after all the Lord Jesus that must be presented to people, whether it is the role of confessor, counsellor, or psychotherapist that is being played. To quote Lee again (p. 119):

> The confessor gives overt assurance of forgiveness to the penitent for his misdeeds and sinful attitudes. The counsellor gives no such assurance on behalf of God or the Church, but he lives forgiveness by the way he accepts his client as he is and passes no moral judgement on him.

'Neither do I condemn thee'—it is not for man, not even for the

Son of man, to anticipate the verdict of God : he must live forgiveness. But the Lord himself gave overt assurance of forgiveness when he said, 'Your sins are forgiven'—he did not tell people that their sins were not sins, or that they could not have done otherwise. And though he did not condemn the individual sinner, he did say, 'Go and sin no more'. Condemning the sin but not the sinner is not so foolish a maxim; the danger comes when condemnation of the sin is thought to be condemnation of that whole area of life from which the sin comes—as though the wrongness of fornication involved the wrongness of sexual relations, and as though salvation meant a suppression of the body and its desires.

Lee's book on counselling is particularly valuable for its warnings to the priest and to any counsellor to know himself. It is comparatively easy for the priest to know himself to be a fellow sinner—the probability is that he himself is in the habit of making his confession. What is far more difficult is for him to know himself to be sick, to be the victim of repressions and to be influenced by unconscious motives, which are responsible not merely for some minor eccentricities of conduct but, it may be, for his very 'uprightness' and inflexibility of purpose. The priest is far more 'conditioned' than he realizes, whether psychologically or by his environment. Let him not run away from the pain of this discovery, and his ability to be of service to others will be greatly enlarged.

IV
SITUATION ETHICS

Some readers of this book will feel that much of the argument is based on an outworn premise. They have learned from Joseph Fletcher's *Situation Ethics* that there is nothing intrinsically right and nothing intrinsically wrong—with one exception : to act lovingly, i.e. for the benefit of the majority, is always right; and always wrong is, not hating, as might have been supposed, but not caring, the attitude of detached indifference. To reach this conclusion, Fletcher erects two dummies and has little difficulty in knocking them down. One approach, he says, is the legalist one, to start with some moral absolutes (the Ten Commandments or something similar) and then deduce from them one's moral duties in daily life. This, he rightly observes, leads to Pharisaism and (in the bad sense of the word) casuistry. Opposed to this is antinomianism, the refusal to admit the validity of moral laws, and trusting instead to one's own moral insights or illuminations (or, as with Sartre, requiring authentic freedom-affirming decisions which do not proceed from, but themselves create, his personality). This he easily shows to be anti-Christian and irresponsible. Therefore all should subscribe to situation ethics.

Love (which translates *agape* and not anything else) must be the Christian's only absolute standard. Fletcher's disciple in preparing for confession would ask himself the one question, Have I failed to show *agape* in my dealings with others? He might confess, as all do, to selfishness in his dealings with others; he might confess that he had observed a moral law, e.g. that he had failed to commit adultery, though he had since come to realize that he should have, he might also confess that he had been largely automatic in doing what were considered 'right actions', i.e. that he had lived by a 'Christian' code of moral behaviour instead of deliberately seeking to show *agape* in all that he said and did.

Even the old-fashioned confessor would not find this penitent too difficult to deal with. The first group of offences would be the sins to which he was accustomed; and as regards the third group, he would not for the first time explain that the Christian way of life was a great deal more than avoiding wrong behaviour, and that all one's good actions needed to be supernaturalized so that they became the work of the indwelling Saviour. And even with the second group of sins, the priest might elucidate the position by pointing out 'the greatest treason: to do the right deed for the wrong reason',[3] and that it was indeed sinful to harden one's heart against a fellow creature. But to do the wrong deed for the right reason would have been hardly satisfactory either; and the right deed for the right reason was to be preferred to either. And he would endeavour to show that consideration for others in the widest sense precluded the particular course of action envisaged.

For situation ethics, as described by Fletcher, is no such third option as he imagines. It is bound either to become the 'legalistic' position, transformed by what he recognizes to be the usual person-centred casuistry; and much of what he propounds is the accepted way in which the confessor sets about his business; or it falls into the antinomian or the sentimentalist attitude which whitewashes sin in the name of love.

* T. S. Eliot, *Murder in the Cathedral* (Faber 1935), p. 44.

As a careful reading of his book will show, Fletcher is aware that (on his assessment) Jesus was not sufficiently consistent in his situation ethics; he is aware that a bit more substance needs to be given to his one essential maxim (e.g. that *agape* shown towards a lot of people is to be preferred to *agape* shown to a few); he is perhaps aware too that Jesus gave a good deal of ethical teaching and did not merely reiterate the command, *Love*. And however firmly he put love in the foreground, it did not lead him to repudiate the validity of the Decalogue. Far from qualifying the command not to commit adultery, Jesus intensified it by forbidding the deliberate encouragement of the desire. But perhaps Fletcher's chief failure is that he has at the centre of his thinking *agape* rather than him in whom *agape* is seen to the fullest possible extent. It is the daily companionship with Jesus and the guidance of his Spirit that illuminates and strengthens; and it is the longing for the closer walk with God that redeems ethics from the taint of priggishness.

1

An instruction on confession

SUGGESTIONS FOR COMMENDING THE PRACTICE

1. Make it clear that the purpose of confession is not only to 'wipe the slate clean' but also to strengthen the Christian's faith-relationship with his Lord and to help him become more aware of his Saviour's love for him.

2. Call attention to such passages as Mark 2.5-7 (Jesus forgiving sins), John 20.21-3 (Jesus passing on the power specifically to his disciples), Acts 2.38 (exercise of the power through baptism), 1 Cor. 5.1-5, 2 Cor. 2.10 (binding and loosing of post-baptismal sin).

3. The power has been passed on in the Church. Key references in the Book of Common Prayer (1662) are: the form for ordaining a priest in 'The Ordering of Priests'; 'The Visitation of the Sick' (the sick person to be 'moved to make a special confession of his sins'); 'The Communion' (first exhortation after the Prayer for the Church, last paragraph).

4. The Anglican approach to the question of obligation is summed up: 'All may, none must, some should'. The question that the individual should ask himself is, 'Have I good reason for thinking that I am not in the last category?' or, 'What does Jesus my Lord and Saviour want me to do?'

THE A B C OF CONFESSION

A—ASK God to help you to see your sins. Use the collect for Whit Sunday or Trinity 19. Test yourself in the light of Scripture passages such as Matt. 5.3-10 (the beatitudes); Romans 12.8-14; 1 Cor. 13; Gal. 5.13-26. Write down your failures, including the good things you could have done and didn't do.

B—BE SORRY for your sins, above all for your ingratitude to God and for your share in crucifying Jesus. You can *be* sorry by acknowledging your sins and trying to do better: this is more important than *feeling* sorry.

C—CONFESS. There is no need to be frightened. The priest will not think less of you (if he knows you already) nor will he be shocked. He will never speak to anyone of anything he hears in confession. It is to Jesus that you are making confession, and it is his forgiveness that you receive. Be very open, frank and receptive.

D—DO BETTER. After advice and absolution the priest will ask you to do a penance (e.g. saying a prayer or reading a short passage from the Bible privately) as a token of your desire to respond to God's loving reconciliation of you with him. Don't be discouraged by subsequent failures or lapses. Jesus said that we are to forgive one another 'seventy times seven' (i.e. infinitely: Matt. 18.21-35). God's love for us is inexhaustible.

A good thanksgiving for absolution is Psalm 103.1-13.

SOME OBJECTIONS ANSWERED

Can't I be forgiven without this?

Yes, of course, just as God can give you strength apart from Holy Communion. But if confession is in any sense of the word 'sacramental' it can be a means of grace and 'a pledge to assure us thereof' (Prayer Book, Catechism). The more conscientious you are, the more you doubt whether you are really forgivable, and therefore you may well need this pledge or assurance.

Isn't it an exclusively Roman Catholic practice?

No, for it is practised in the Holy Orthodox Church and to some small extent among the reformed churches of the West. In the Church of England there have always been some, since the Reformation, who have practised it. It is one of the great spiritual and moral opportunities open to all Christians willing to avail themselves of it.

Why should a priest come between me and God?

Suppose you were asked the same question with the word 'Bible' substituted for 'priest': you would say that the Bible was a help, not a barrier, and that it makes the love of God more real to you. So with the priest in confession.

Priests are sinners like everyone else.

Certainly, but in hearing confessions they are ministers of Christ. It is not their own forgiveness they pass on, but Christ's.

I see no point in confessing and then going and doing the same things again.

Agreed—if you mean confessing with the deliberate intention of doing the same things again. No—if you mean confessing and fearing that sooner or later you may do the same thing again. By owning up, and bringing our weakness to Christ ('Just as I am ...') our will can become stronger and our readiness to resist temptation (really, Christ's will in us, and Christ's power in us) greater. A very great deal in this, as in all matters of morality, depends upon intention and purpose. But Christ knows, better than we know ourselves, how feeble, divided and incomplete these can be. 'The goodness of God is the highest prayer, and it comes down to the lowest part of our need' (Julian of Norwich, *Revelations of Divine Love*, ch. vi).

APPENDIX

2

Suggestions for further reading

'Forasmuch then as your office is both of so great excellency and of
so great difficulty, ye see with how great care and study ye ought to
apply yourselves ... to beware, that neither you yourselves offend,
nor be occasion that others offend.' These words from the Ordering
of Priests apply especially to that part of the priest's ministry which
has to do with the ministry to the penitent. Robust common sense,
valuable as it is, is for the medical practitioner no substitute for hard
study; and though it is no less valuable for the priest, it is far from
being the only prerequisite for the hearing of confessions. The following is a select list of books which may be of help to the priest who
hears confessions. It presupposes the study of bible and doctrine, and
in particular of the theology of forgiveness in such classical works as
H. R. Mackintosh, *The Christian Experience of Forgiveness* (published
1927, now a Fontana paperback) and O. C. Quick, *The Gospel of the
New World* (1944). Among recent books J. Macquarrie, *Principles
of Christian Theology* (SCM 1966) or J. A. Baker, *The Foolishness
of God* (Darton, Longman and Todd 1970) should serve to freshen
the priest's ideas on Christian doctrine.

ETHICS

Though it does not help the confessor directly, the study of Ethics is
extremely important, if only to prevent him falling victim to passing
crazes. A. C. Ewing, *Ethics* (English Universities Press 1953) provides
a simple and absorbing guide to the subject. There is much of
indirect value to the confessor in J. Wilson, N. Williams, and B.
Sugarman, *Introduction to Moral Education* (Penguin 1968); if forces
him to consider the purpose he is seeking to achieve in his training
of others.

MORAL THEOLOGY

The works of K. E. Kirk are almost indispensable reading for the
Anglican priest: *Some Principles of Moral Theology* (1920), *Ignor-*

ance, Faith and Conformity (1925), *Conscience and its Problems* (1927). More recent works along traditional lines are R. C. Mortimer, *The Elements of Moral Theology* (Black 1947) and H. M. Waddams, *A New Introduction to Moral Theology* (SCM 1964). For the earlier post-Reformation Anglican tradition, see H. R. McAdoo, *The Structure of Caroline Moral Theology* (Longmans 1949), T. Wood, *English Casuistical Divinity during the Seventeenth Century* (SPCK 1952) and C. F. Allison, *The Rise of Moralism* (SPCK 1966). Standard Roman Catholic books are H. Davis, *Moral and Pastoral Theology*, 4 vols (Sheed and Ward Inc., New York, 2e. 1936); J. A. McHugh and C. J. Callan, *Moral Theology*, 2 vols, rev. E. P. Farrell (Joseph F. Wagner Inc., New York, 1958); and, for a less juridical and scholastic approach, B. Häring, *The Law of Christ*, 3 vols (Newman Press, Westminster, Md., 1964—). See also K. Rahner, *Theological Investigations*, vol. ii (Darton, Longman and Todd 1961), pp. 135-74, 'Forgotten Truths concerning the Sacrament of Penance'; J. Fitzsimons, ed., *Penance: Virtue and Sacrament* (Search Press 1969) and G. Hagmaier and R. W. Gleason, *Moral Problems Now* (Sheed and Ward 1960) for fresh approaches from within Roman Catholicism. A stimulating contribution from a Methodist theologian is H. McKeating, *Living with Guilt* (SCM 1970).

SITUATION ETHICS

Ethical principles have always to be applied to circumstances, as many of the books already mentioned show. J. Fletcher, *Situation Ethics* (SCM 1966), comes close to denying the propriety of studying ethics at all. The pros and cons can be studied in Outka and Ramsey (editors), *Norm and Context in Christian Ethics* (SCM 1969). Also useful are H. Oppenheimer, *The Character of Christian Morality* (Faith Press 1965) and P. Lehmann, *Ethics in a Christian Context* (Harper and Row, New York, 1963). There is a magisterial survey of the whole field in N. H. G. Robinson, *The Groundwork of Christian Ethics* (Collins 1971).

THE SPIRITUAL LIFE

The best modern writing, from all parts of the Church, makes no sharp distinction between 'Moral', 'Ascetic', and 'Mystical' Theology. Among older books which can still help the confessor to advise penitents about prayer may be mentioned F. P. Harton, *Elements of the Spiritual Life* (SPCK 1932), H. Northcott, *The Venture of Prayer* (SPCK 1950), and R. Cant, *Christian Prayer* (Faith Press 1961). Recent books which take serious account of the intellectual climate from the mid-60s on are E. James, ed., *Spirituality for Today* (SCM

1967), H. Rack, *Twentieth Century Spirituality* (Epworth 1969) and J. Dalrymple, *The Christian Affirmation* (Darton, Longman and Todd 1971). There is a very impressive restatement of traditional ascetic teaching in A. Squire, *Asking the Fathers* (SPCK 1973).

HISTORY

Historical works which contain much valuable guidance both for confessor and penitent are O. D. Watkins, *A History of Penance*, 2 vols (1920, reprinted 1961), K. E. Kirk, *The Vision of God* (1931), R. C. Mortimer, *The Origins of Private Penance in the Western Church* (1939), W. Telfer, *The Forgiveness of Sins* (SCM 1959), P. F. Palmer, ed., *Sacraments and Forgiveness*, Sources of Christian Theology, vol. ii (Newman Press, Westminster, Md., 1960), B. Poschmann, *Penance and the Anointing of the Sick* (Herder 1964), J. Gunstone, *The Liturgy of Penance* (Faith Press 1966).

Among books designed to help confessors, F. G. Belton, *A Manual for Confessors* (Mowbray 1916) did good service in its generation and gave a simplified version of the current Roman Catholic approach. It was disappointing that *A Guide for Spiritual Directors* by 'The Author of *The Way*' (Mowbray 1957) should prove so idiosyncratic. The author was a much loved and trusted spiritual director and what he wrote always deserved consideration. An unpretentious simple Roman Catholic paperback which has much that is valuable in it is G. Kelly, *The Good Confessor* (Clonmore and Reynolds 1955) and A. Wilson, *Pardon and Peace* (Sheed and Ward 1954) is very practical. But the full effects of Vatican II and the *Humanae Vitae* controversy have yet to appear.

For the help of penitents, in addition to books already mentioned, W. L. Knox, *Penitence and Forgiveness* (SPCK 1951), P. D. Butterfield, *How To Make Your Confession* (SPCK 1952) and E. James, *The Double Cure* (Hodder 1957) may be commended. Disappointingly negative, but with good positive insights, is J. R. W. Stott, *Confess Your Sins* (Hodder 1964) from a Conservative Evangelical standpoint.

As an immediate preparation for hearing confessions, the traditional rules as adapted and translated in Walter Carey, *My Priesthood* (pp. 90-5), are useful. And if a model of wise spiritual counsel is desired, it is hard to improve on the writings of St Francis of Sales, notably his *Introduction to the Devout Life*: this is a book which a priest may well use for his own edification while keeping the time appointed for hearing confessions.

Index